"As a pastor, professor, and apologist, I am thankful for the work done by Hartman and McEwen in *Pastor as Apologist*. It is a reminder that the earliest practitioners of apologetics were clergy, not just specialists in the guild. It is a call for pastors to reclaim that for the good of the church and the communities they serve. To that end, *Pastor as Apologist* also provides thoughts on how to incorporate apologetics into the life of the church through discipleship and sermons, while keeping your eye on the centrality of Scripture in the process. It is readable, practical, and forging a path forward for reclaiming a practice that is important in the life of the church for the building up of its people and advancing the reasonableness of our faith."

—**Jeremy Evans**, senior pastor, Woodridge
Baptist Church, Kingwood, Texas

"Dayton Hartman and Michael McEwen do a marvelous job on addressing an often-overlooked issue within our local churches today. Oftentimes pastors and leaders communicate to church members that Christian beliefs and thinking is still the prevalent worldview. We all and always need the gospel to challenge the pillars of our lives that are at times not grounded in the scriptures. Dayton and Michael demonstrate very clearly the necessity and the biblical warrant for apologetics in our local church context today. This book is essential for Christian leaders, equipping them with the necessary skillsets to encourage believers who are regularly faced with perspectives that are counter to the gospel."

—**Douglas A. Logan Jr.**, president of Grimké Seminary

T0035924

"To be Christian involves pursuing and delighting in the truth. The work of the pastor involves not only loving and preaching the truth, but also lovingly proving this truth to the church time and time again. In this book you'll find a winsome invitation to carry out pastoral ministry as an apologist who lovingly eviscerates the lies of the enemy and consistently upholds Jesus—who is himself the truth."

—**Tony Merida**, pastor for preaching and vision,
Imago Dei Church, Raleigh, North Carolina

"Among the many responsibilities of a pastor, the discipline to give a reason for our Christian hope remains central to our preaching, shepherding, and counseling. This, as Hartman and McEwen suggest, is pastoral apologetics. For a discipline that sometimes garners the reputation of mere intellectual defensiveness, Hartman and McEwen offer a winsome and humble approach for pastors that is biblically grounded, historically informed, anchored in the confidence of Christ's resurrection, and highly practical. As a seminary professor and pastor, I'm thrilled to see such a helpful resource to remind and equip pastors in the important task of defending the faith."

—**Benjamin Quinn**, associate professor of theology and
history of ideas and associate director of the Center for Faith
and Culture, Southeastern Baptist Theological Seminary

The PASTOR as APOLOGIST

The PASTOR as APOLOGIST

RESTORING APOLOGETICS TO THE LOCAL CHURCH

DAYTON HARTMAN & MICHAEL MCEWEN

ACADEMIC
BRENTWOOD, TENNESSEE

The Pastor as Apologist: Restoring Apologetics to the Local Church
Copyright © 2024 by Dayton Hartman and Michael McEwen

Published by B&H Academic
Brentwood, Tennessee

ISBN: 978-1-4627-4970-6

Dewey Decimal Classification: 239
Subject Heading: APOLOGETICS \
THEOLOGY \ CHURCH

All Scripture quotations are taken from the Christian Standard
Bible®, Copyright © 2017 by Holman Bible Publishers. Used
by permission. Christian Standard Bible® and CSB® are
federally registered trademarks of Holman Bible Publishers.

The web addresses referenced in this book were live and correct at
the time of the book's publication but may be subject to change.

Cover Credit: Cover design by Matt Lehman. Cover
images Tanu V/Shutterstock and Yarikart/Shutterstock.

Printed in the United States of America

29 28 27 26 25 24 VP 1 2 3 4 5 6 7 8 9 10

DEDICATION

Dayton Hartman
For my wife, Rebekah, who faithfully demonstrates
the gospel to me daily.

Michael McEwen
For Jade, my bride and my co-laborer in all things beautiful.

CONTENTS

ACKNOWLEDGMENTS

Dayton Hartman

I want to express my gratitude to the publishing team at B&H Academic for their belief in this project and their patience with me as I put the manuscript together. I am especially thankful for the grace given to me by Madison Trammel and Michael McEwen.

Michael McEwen

Some of the greatest gifts in life are the ones you least expect. This book was one of those unexpected gifts. I'm deeply grateful to Dayton for inviting me along to cowrite this little primer for pastors who desire to be apologetically thoughtful in the pulpit.

INTRODUCTION

"I hated pastoring!" The air was thick with awkwardness, as I (Dayton) listened to one of my favorite Christian thinkers express his disdain for the pastorate. In a room filled with other seminary students, we remained silent as this tirade continued. This well-known scholar expressed further frustration about the days and hours he wasted by "squabbling over youth group [and] spaghetti fundraiser luncheons rather than spending [his] days doing the serious work of a scholar." Just moments later, this self-professed apologist looked at the seminary students in the room and told us that we should really consider academia rather than ministry in the local church. Still, he said, "Those who pursue pastoral ministry are great people."

In the ensuing moments, he began to backtrack from his pontifications and instead spoke fondly of positive elements of the ministry of the pastor. Nevertheless, the damage was done. It was clear that the implication of these criticisms was that those who are intelligent go into academia and those who are not intellectually gifted will retreat to the menial labor of pastoring.

Numerous students, myself included, began to dream of writing on weighty matters without the burden of the church. To speak at conferences instead of enduring the week-to-week grind of Sunday sermons, funeral services, and weddings. Our appetite for moderated public debates, in which we would valiantly defend the truth claims of Christianity, grew, and our interest in debating the meaningless issues of the local church waned. Over the next year, multiple students expressed a sense of calling away from the pastorate and toward the office of full-time apologist.

Yet the most basic of knowledge regarding the New Testament would betray the fact that nobody is called to the spiritual role of apologist or polemicist. There is no spiritual gifting defined as "Christian Thinker." On the contrary, you see that God's plan for the advancement of the gospel is the local church, and pastors, we believe, are called to help serve the local church in apologetic roles. In addition, a brief survey of church history would reveal that among the early Christians, leadership in the local church was the platform from which apologetic writing, intellectual argumentation, and scholarly engagement were being produced.

Far from the local church being a place of trivial matters and being of secondary importance to robust Christian thinking, the New Testament and church history demonstrate the local church to be the primary institution of Christian intellectual engagement. Rather than philosophers leading the way in the Christian expression of truth, pastors were of primary importance.

Now, well over a decade since the scene I described above, I (Dayton) am a pastor and a professor. I value Christian academia. I thank God for the seminary system and all that it does to raise up and equip Christian leaders. And I love the local church, because I read that Jesus bled and died for the church. The plan to reach the world with the gospel comes via the local church, not the seminaries. Obviously, Christian education, Christian scholars, and seminaries all exist as important handmaidens to the local church. One of the beauties of academia is that it helps raise up Christian scholars who serve in churches, and we're convinced that Christian thinkers are a blessing to the church. However, our aim must be to use Christian universities and seminaries to send scholars into the pastorate, to send thinkers into the mission field. We must reclaim the historic role and biblical mandate for the local church pastor as an apologist.

Chapter 1

Apologetics in Scripture

The Bible never asks us to believe what is not
true. By the same token, one of the principal
ways the Bible increases and strengthens faith
is by articulating and defending the truth.

—D. A. CARSON[1]

Jesus calls believers to love God with all our heart, soul, and mind (Matt 22:37). So Christians, by nature, are to be a thinking people. We are a bookish people who center our lives on

---

[1] D. A. Carson, *Prophetic from the Center* (LaGrange, KY: 10Publishing, 2019), 30.

a written text that is understood through, in some sense, an intellectual pursuit.[2] Our love for our God is not only an emotive action, but also an intellectual pursuit, an ongoing thirst for increased knowledge and intimacy with the God of the gospel.

Defining Our Terms: "Apologetics" can be defined in a variety of ways. Some scholars opt for more aggressive-sounding definitions that manifest themselves in some variation of the following words: a defense of the truth claims of Christianity. While that is accurate, we prefer John Frame's positive and biblical definition. He says that apologetics is "the discipline that teaches Christians how to give a reason for their hope." We would argue that this more positive approach to defining apologetics better captures the essence and tone of the biblical mandate.

John Frame, *Apologetics: A Justification of Christian Belief* (Phillipsburg, NJ: P&R, 2015), 1.

In this chapter, our goal is twofold: First, we want to illustrate how the words of Scripture can guide us into a biblical landscape of apologetics and apologetic living. For example, learning from

---

[2] Larry W. Hurtado, *Destroyer of the Gods: Early Christian Distinctiveness in the Roman World* (Waco, TX: Baylor, 2016), 105.

the apostle Peter, we are convinced that apologetics is a humble yet honest demonstration of the truths of Scripture in winsome and holistic ways. As you will see in what follows, apologetics isn't just a defense with our words, but also a defense with our whole selves. Secondly, we will connect these thoughts to the role and responsibilities of the pastor, the one who is called to model apologetics for his congregation. These two areas will establish a foundation for the rest of our work, especially chapters 3 and 4, where we offer principles and practices for apologetics in your local church.

Thinking Christians in a Hostile World

It is helpful to begin by contextualizing Peter's call for the church to "give a defense" for their faith in light of the political and social persecution Christians experienced at the time of Peter's epistle. Nero's reign (AD 37–68) was largely marked by a hate-filled aggression toward the Christian faith. Blaming the Christians for a destructive fire in Rome, Nero responded with murderous fury, lighting Christians on fire and using their burning corpses to light the streets of Rome.[3] It was in this context that Peter penned his letter to the churches in Rome, which were increasingly

---

[3] For a fuller narrative of Nero's disgust, see the Roman historian Tacitus's book *Annals*. Instead of painting an unblemished picture of Emperor Nero, Tacitus states that Nero "falsely charged with guilt, and punished with the most fearful tortures, the persons commonly called Christians, who were hated for their enormities" (*Annals* 15.44).

facing government-sanctioned hostility. Peter's letter describes how Christians ought to respond to hostile neighbors and widespread persecution. The key text for apologetics is in 1 Pet 3:15:

> Who then will harm you if you are devoted to what is good? But even if you should suffer for righteousness, you are blessed. Do not fear them or be intimidated, but in your hearts regard Christ the Lord as holy, ready at any time to give a defense to anyone who asks you for a reason for the hope that is in you. Yet do this with gentleness and reverence, keeping a clear conscience, so that when you are accused, those who disparage your good conduct in Christ will be put to shame. (1 Pet 3:13–16)

In these three verses, Peter wants the early church to see its faith within the larger narrative of Christ's suffering, which animates who they are and how they are to respond to these social conflicts. Let's explore the three verses in more detail:

"**. . . in your hearts regard Christ the Lord as holy . . .**" The first step in an apologetic defense comes long before any kind of intellectual challenge arises. The building blocks of an apologetic argument begin with the lordship of Jesus. We cannot defend a faith we do not live, and we do not live our faith unless the lordship of Jesus is evident in our lives. The place where this evidence is most clearly manifested is a relentless pursuit of holiness.

Although from a different apostle and epistle, Paul writes, carrying the same driving point, "If the dead are not raised, 'Let us eat and drink, for tomorrow we die.' Do not be deceived: 'Bad company corrupts good morals.' Come to your senses and stop sinning; for some people are ignorant about God. I say this to your shame" (1 Cor 15:32–34). The reality of Jesus's resurrection is an impetus for the church's way of being in the world. If the church adopts an Epicurean lifestyle of hedonistic pleasure ("eat, drink, and be merry"), it's living a lifestyle contrary to the new creation Christ has inaugurated through his resurrection. In short, the resurrection generates a holy-and-holistic apologetic that echoes Christ's life, death, and resurrection.

"**. . . ready at any time to give a defense (*apologia*) . . .**" Peter invites believers to be prepared to make a legal defense. The English word *defense* is a translation from the Greek word *apologia*. New Testament scholar Craig Keener writes, "Being able to offer a defense meant being able to show that the charges against Christians (or at least against the Christian movement as a whole) were untrue."[4] In the historical context we highlighted earlier, Peter's advice makes perfect sense. According to Tacitus, Nero had "falsely charged" Christians with rioting and other treasonous crimes that deserved persecution and punishment.

Acknowledging these false accusations in his epistle (see 2:12 and 3:16, for example), Peter pastorally nudges them to "live in such

---

[4] Craig Keener, "Lifestyle Apologetics and 1 Peter 3:15," Bible Background, July 1, 2019, https://craigkeener.com/lifestyle-apologetics-and-1-peter-315/.

a way that refutes such accusations, at least among those who know you personally."[5]

Legal defenses require more than pithy statements and bumper-sticker slogans. Rather, legal arguments must be clear, cogent, logical, and compelling as the one making the argument demonstrates a commanding knowledge of the subject being discussed. Thus, Peter is insisting that once we live as if Christ is Lord, we will pursue a thorough and intimate knowledge of him that can be stated, defended, and lived with confidence. While Peter does not accuse those who are unable to make a robust defense of their faith as having rejected the lordship of Christ, we could argue that a submission to the lordship of Christ will necessarily manifest itself in an ability to state, explain, and defend Christ as Lord.

". . . Yet do this with gentleness and respect . . ." Sadly, much apologetic engagement is bent on winning arguments rather than winning souls (to borrow old-school Baptist language).[6] Peter's

---

[5] Keener.

[6] To clarify the term *soul*, we are not advocating for a faulty anthropological dualism where soul and body are utterly detached from one another. Various camps of American fundamentalism have unfortunately advocated for an unhealthy Platonism where the soul (an immaterial, unblemished kernel) is more worthy of the church's attention than the body (a material, fleshly, blemished shell). Rather, when we speak of *soul*, we're focused on what Karl Barth calls the "ensouled body" or "embodied soul." We believe these categories better describe what it means to be human because such descriptions value God's original creation while also upholding two other doctrines, such as the incarnation and new creation.

admonishment is meant to recall our minds back to the lordship of Christ. If your defense of the faith is grounded in the lordship of Jesus, then you will treat those being pursued by Jesus (unbelievers or skeptics) with a kind of dignity and respect that reveals Christ's love for them. This is especially important in an age when much of the interactions on Twitter and other media platforms could be described as trolling. Christians must never participate in unfair, unfounded, provocative interactions simply meant to win the exchange or elicit a frustrated response from the one with whom we are interacting.

The two Greek terms Peter uses are *prautēs* and *phobos*. The first is only found in letters written by Paul, Peter, and James, and it denotes meekness and humble consideration, and by the latter, Peter means a reverent respect. But notice how Peter uses both terms in connection with our relational intentions and interactions with others. These terms carry traces of the life and ministry of Jesus, which is largely Peter's point: "In this way, once again Peter underscores that Christian comportment in relation to those who bear malice toward Christians is determined by the fundamental orientation of one's life toward God, by according the highest value to one's relationship with God with the result that it determines all else."[7]

---

[7] Joel B. Green, *1 Peter*, The Two Horizons New Testament Commentary (Grand Rapids: Eerdmans, 2007), 118.

For Peter, engaging objections and inquiries with gentleness and respect assumes an intimate knowledge of God's grace, mercy, and compassion discovered in and through the work and person of Jesus.

Contending for the Gospel

In the famed exhortation by the half-brother of Jesus, Jude, the apostle writes, "Dear friends, although I was eager to write you about the salvation we share, I found it necessary to write, appealing to you to contend for the faith that was delivered to the saints once for all" (1:3). What is notable about Jude's words is not that we contend for truth, but the content of the truth for which we must contend.

In distinction from Peter—who is dealing with misrepresentations of Christianity—Jude addresses the false teaching that had arisen in some churches. Those false teachers had stealthily come in and were twisting the nature of grace. Thus, Jude's command is not to defend a mere set of truth propositions, but the gospel itself. This necessarily leads to two points worth exploring.

First, to defend the content of the gospel message, we must explicitly define the gospel message. Following the advice of Tony Merida, all preaching, and especially the preaching of the gospel, should be typified by "simplicity and clarity."[8] The gospel begins

---

[8] Tony Merida, *Faithful Preaching: Declaring Scripture with Responsibility, Passion, and Authenticity* (Nashville: B&H Academic, 2009), 172.

Notable Quotes: Writing about the evangelical love affair with anti-intellectualism, philosopher Os Guinness has correctly summarized the condition of the American church: "We are a people with a true, sometimes a deep, experience of God. But we are no longer a people of truth. Only rarely are we serious about theology at a popular level. We are still suspicious of thinking and scholarship. We are still attracted to movements that replace thinking and theology by other emphases—relational, therapeutic, charismatic, and managerial (as in church growth)."

Os Guinness, *Fit Bodies, Fat Minds: Why Evangelicals Don't Think and What to Do About It* (Grand Rapids: Baker, 1994), 38.

with bad news: we are sinners who have broken the infinitely good laws of the infinitely good God of heaven. As a result, we owe God an infinite debt. As finite creatures, we lack the means necessary to pay that debt. However, God has not left us on our own. Instead, he sent the eternal Son of God (Jesus of Nazareth) to be born of a virgin, to live a perfect and sinless life in our place, and to die the sinner's death that we deserve. The death of the infinitely holy Son of God, in the place of finite sinners, is sufficient to pay the debt of all sinners who repent and believe the gospel. And the evidence that the work of Jesus was and is sufficient for sinners is that three days after his death, Jesus physically arose from the dead.

Second, Jude's exhortation assumes that the central claim of Christianity, which is summarized in the gospel, is true. As a result, any contending for the faith must begin with the conviction that Christianity is true.[9] No one contends for what is false; rather, we contend for what is true, and as Scripture teaches, God's truth is not neutral. God is rightly biased toward what is good, true, and beautiful, and by nature, he is opposed to evil, falsehoods, and ugliness.

> **Notable Quotes:** "Christianity can never be separated from some theory about the existence and the nature of God. The result is that Christian theism must be thought of as a unit."
>
> ──────────
>
> Cornelius Van Til, *Christian Apologetics*, ed. William Edgar (Phillipsburg, NJ: P&R, 2003), 19.

──────────

[9] We differ on this point from the authors of the excellent book *Stand Firm*. They write, "In making a defense, the Christian apologist makes no explicit Christian assumptions; for example, she doesn't assume Scripture is true and simply appeal to a chapter and verse in defense of Christianity's claims." Paul Gould, Travis Dickinson, Keith Loftin, *Stand Firm: Apologetics and the Brilliance of the Gospel* (Nashville: B&H Academic, 2018), 3.

Cornelius Van Til (1895–1987) was a Christian philosopher who advocated for what we call presuppositionalist apologetics. Van Til was pushing back against certain philosophical categories originating in modernity that conceded truth as neutral, and since it was supposedly neutral, everyone had access to it via his or her reason. Drawing from the vantage point of Scripture, Van Til stated that scriptural truth isn't neutral, whether found in implicit or explicit assumptions of Scripture. For Van Til, all of life and thought is a duel between Christian and non-Christian philosophies of life, and Scripture reveals the truest reality of God, the world, and ourselves, which means that all other perspectives are fragmented, futile, or false.[10]

Romans 1, a text we will examine next, is the biblical ground where Van Til noticed this friction between Christian and non-Christian epistemologies.

---

[10] Cornelius Van Til, *Christian Apologetics*, ed. William Edgar (Phillipsburg, NJ: P&R, 2003), 17. I (Dayton) do believe that Francis Schaeffer and John Frame, self-described presuppositional thinkers, have the right approach to these issues by adopting a form of modified-presuppositional apologetics, which recognizes the need for contextualization. A guiding principle, regardless of one's preferred apologetic methodology, should be convictionally committed to contextualization because "culture is never stagnant, changing and adapting as ideas evolve, and this means that all apologetics is contextual." Benjamin K. Forrest, Joshua D. Chatraw, and Alister E. McGrath, eds., *The History of Apologetics: A Biographical and Methodological Introduction* (Grand Rapids: Zondervan Academic, 2020), 23.

They Became Fools

In his theological masterpiece, Romans, the apostle Paul argues that the guilt of humanity is evident.

> For God's wrath is revealed from heaven against all godless-ness and unrighteousness of people who by their unrigh-teousness suppress the truth, since what can be known about God is evident among them, because God has shown it to them. (Rom 1:18–19)

The natural bent of the human heart is to suppress truth. In *Lies Pastors Believe*, I (Dayton) attempted to state this fact in a way that would be easily digested and accepted:

> Only a miracle stops us from being drawn to lies. As Christians, this shouldn't surprise us. Every time we sin, we believe lies: We believe that God is not good, he does not love us, and he has not met our greatest need. Our hearts, apart from God's regenerating grace, are lie-producing and lie-believing machines (Jer 17:9). As sinners, you could say that lies are our native language.[11]

Since this is true, then all use of truth by unbelievers borrows from God's truth. This makes sense of the nature of knowledge

---

[11] Dayton Hartman, *Lies Pastors Believe: Seven Ways to Elevate Yourself, Subvert the Gospel, and Undermine the Church* (Bellingham, WA: Lexham, 2017), 2.

Notable Quotes: John Chrysostom (347–407) said, "God has placed the knowledge of himself in human hearts from the beginning. But this knowledge they unwisely invested in wood and stone and thus contaminated the truth, at least as far as they were able. Meanwhile the truth abides unchanged, having its own unchanging glory. . . . How did God reveal himself? By a voice from heaven? Not at all! God made a panoply which was able to draw them more than by a voice. He put before them the immense creation, so that both the wise and the unlearned, the Scythian and the barbarian, might ascend to God, having learned through sight the beauty of the things which they had seen."

John Chrysostom, "Homilies of St. John Chrysostom, Archbishop of Constantinople, on the Epistle of St. Paul to the Romans," in *Saint Chrysostom: Homilies on the Acts of the Apostles and the Epistle to the Romans*, ed. Philip Schaff, trans. J. B. Morris, W. H. Simcox, and George B. Stevens, vol. 11, A Select Library of the Nicene and Post-Nicene Fathers of the Christian Church, First Series (New York: Christian Literature Company, 1889), 351.

in general. All that can be learned by humans is already known by God. Thus, all human knowledge that corresponds to reality is derivative knowledge. In other words, we derive all knowledge from the mind of God, a being who already knows all things. Since knowledge is derivative by nature, the use of knowledge by the unbeliever must be coupled with a conscious or subconscious effort to suppress some aspect of truth—chiefly, that all knowledge comes from the Creator. The Christian defense of truth must be distinctly Christian in orientation because truth itself is distinctly Christian. Otherwise, we allow the possibility that the non-Christian philosophy of life being used by unbelievers is a viable interaction with truth.[12] Scripture makes it clear that it is not.

The Pastor-Apologist

This conversation demonstrates the need for apologetic engagement. So what does this have to do with pastors? Aren't these matters for philosophers to be concerned with rather than the pastor in the pulpit? In short, no. Paul lists apologetics as a task of the pastor for which a man who is aspiring to the office of elder must be able to navigate.

---

[12] Presuppositional apologist Greg Bahnsen (1948–1995) stated it this way: "We are saying that they do not know anything '*truly*,' because they do not recognize the most fundamental reality: All facts are God-created facts, not brute facts. Things do not simply exist as the result of random evolutionary forces. They are given meaning and significance because they exist in God's plan, for His purpose, and in order to bring Him glory. Indeed, unbelievers do not acknowledge the biggest fact of all reality—God." Gary DeMar, ed., *Pushing the Antithesis: The Apologetic Methodology of Greg L. Bahnsen* (Powder Springs, GA: American Vision, 2007), 32.

As an overseer of God's household, he must be blameless, not arrogant, not hot-tempered, not an excessive drinker, not a bully, not greedy for money, but hospitable, loving what is good, sensible, righteous, holy, self-controlled, *holding to the faithful message as taught, so that he will be able both to encourage with sound teaching and to refute those who contradict it.* (Titus 1:7–9, emphasis added)

An elder, by position and prescription, must have the ability to defend the gospel and to discern, engage, and refute lies. The apologetic task is one of the responsibilities of the pastor. The New Testament envisions churches full of apologists, led by apologists. If we want to curtail the evangelical lurch away from objective truth and scriptural convictions, pastors must lead the way and set the pace in the pursuit of truth.

We must know the gospel, preach the gospel, and defend the gospel. We must love Scripture, preach Scripture, and expose the meaning of Scripture to our people. We must teach our congregations how to read Scripture. If we want the members of our church to stop abandoning truth in the pursuit of feelings and false cultural philosophies, then we must stop abdicating our responsibility to love, preach, and defend truth.

While Christian thinkers, apologists, and philosophers in the academy are wonderful gifts of grace, they are not the first nor even final line of defense for Christian truth claims. Church history demonstrates that the phenomenon of professional apologists is

Notable Quotes: "The Bible . . . knows nothing of preaching divorced from the needed work of persuasion. The two words *preach* and *persuade*, and the two ideas behind them, are indissoluble—most prominently in the tireless work of St. Paul, who was an apologist everywhere he went. He preached and persuaded. He persuaded and preached, and no one can drive so much as the beam of a laser between the two."

Os Guinness, *Fool's Talk: Recovering the Art of Christian Persuasion* (Downers Grove, IL: InterVarsity, 2015), 112.

predominantly modern. For instance, the rise of secularism, mainly in European universities in the Middle Ages,[13] unintentionally catalyzed the call of professional apologetics—a field distinctly separated from particular ecclesiologies. Many early universities, James Axtell points out, "belonged to monasteries, towns, and cathedral towns."[14] As these infant institutions matured, more faculty and new specializations were needed, especially in light of growing scientific discoveries. As modernity dawned, theological training became

---

[13] For a larger genealogical account of the modern university, see James Axtell, *Wisdom's Workshop: The Rise of the Modern University* (Princeton, NJ: Princeton, 2016).

[14] Axtell, 3.

more distanced from the church and more closely entangled with the university, thus making apologetics a more professionalized role directly affiliated with universities. Yet, in the next chapter, we will argue that the defense of the faith has historically been the work of churchmen, not public intellectuals.

Preaching Apologetics

Moving beyond modernity and into our current cultural age, many have described it as increasingly "post-Christian"[15]—a term that requires serious analysis that is unfortunately beyond the scope of our present work. But let us note this: Post-Christianity is an age that attempts to intentionally promote ideologies and narratives counter to Christianity, and in telling such alternative perspectives, these ideas and narratives inculcate desires and beliefs that conflict with the Scriptures. In short, many post-Christian perspectives teach people to love and know reality beyond the stories and symbols of Christianity.[16] Again, such an analysis is beyond the

---

[15] For a few different analyses of the term *post-Christian*, see Gene Edward Veith Jr., *Post-Christian: A Guide to Contemporary Thought and Culture* (Wheaton, IL: Crossway, 2020).

[16] Anyone familiar with the last 150 years of philosophy can see post-Christianity as representing the *Geist* of Friedrich Nietzsche, an infamous, late-nineteenth-century figure whose writings pushed his contemporaries to think and live without the "hauntings" of Western Christianity. Thus, we're intentionally emphasizing the preposition *beyond*—in the way Nietzsche did in his work *Beyond Good and Evil*—as an attempt to shift

boundaries of the current work, yet we will occasionally illustrate throughout this book how and why we can preach apologetically to a post-Christian culture.

In this sense of the word, the Western world has become post-Christian, and churches are having to rapidly adapt to a culture that sees and senses the world without the lens and hands of Scripture.[17] As mentioned earlier, the church was loosely tied to apologetics in the Middle Ages, yet the relationship between the pastorate and apologetics became nearly untethered in modernity, reserved primarily as a professional task. Now, in our post-Christian context, we are suggesting that the church becomes the fertile ground of apologetics, passionately led and implemented by the pastor.

To properly handle such a responsibility today, we must look to our spiritual past in the life of the early church. In Acts, we discover that the apostles themselves preached apologetically in a pre-Christian yet wildly religious environment. These apostles laid bare the truth claims of Jesus and then defended those claims in the very

---

philosophical and cultural trends beyond their present usages to irrupt new ideas, practices, and stories. We're convinced that Nietzsche's hope has been inaugurated, especially in America as terms, concepts, ideas, and beliefs are being questioned and transfigured to fit within influential narratives and ideologies.

[17] For a healthy analysis of understanding our post-Christian age, see Justin Ariel Bailey, *Reimagining Apologetics: The Beauty of Faith in a Secular Age* (Downers Grove, IL: IVP Academic, 2020) and his *Interpreting Your World: Five Lenses for Engaging Theology and Culture* (Grand Rapids: Baker Academic, 2022).

same sermons.[18] In short, if the apostles found the need to defend or support the claims of Jesus in the pre-Christian world, perhaps we should do the same in a post-Christian world.

Additionally, Scripture itself is apologetic in orientation. Old Testament scholars have long argued that the Pentateuch acted as a type of apologetic against the claims and stories that dominated the pagan ancient Near East.[19] If the text of Scripture, which is what we preach, and the pattern of the apostles themselves are oriented toward apologetically engaging the unbelieving world in which they are found, we have good grounding to say that contemporary preaching should be apologetic in nature.[20]

The pastor-apologist must be willing to labor in not only reading Scripture well, but also reading culture well. If the gospel is transcultural, one aim of preaching Scripture is to demonstrate the profundity of the gospel for our cultural moment. It's not that the gospel has power (Rom 1:16–17); that is obviously true. It is also that the gospel has the power to transform people despite their rebellious hearts and renegade worldviews. So when we take time to eviscerate and investigate the cultural teachings and practices of our day, the easier the task will be to plant gospel seeds to

---

[18] E.g., Acts 5; 15; 18.

[19] See, for example, John D. Currid, *Against the Gods* (Wheaton, IL: Crossway, 2013).

[20] This is a subject I explore in chapter 4 of my (Dayton's) book *Church History for Modern Ministry: Why Our Past Matters for Everything We Do* (Bellingham, WA: Lexham, 2016).

allow the Spirit to water and generate life from within our post-Christian terrain.

In this chapter, we introduced a few key concepts and a brief methodology to help you engage in the conversation of preaching apologetically. For us, understanding our concerns while naming the problems are essential before interacting with the history of pastoral apologetics (chapter 2) and putting a pastoral apologetics into practice (chapters 3 and 4). Our aim throughout the book is to demonstrate why apologetics is both a pastoral role and an indispensable responsibility for discipling congregations to give gentle yet persuasive defenses for Jesus's gospel.

Heart Work (Reflection Questions)

1. Does your approach to studying and preaching Scripture demonstrate a high view of its authority?
2. What needs to change in your proclamation of the truth claims of Scripture?
3. What elements of your church's mission and vision are grounded more in entertainment than truth?
4. How can you better prepare your church to interact with the unbelieving world's suppression of truth?

Chapter 2

Apologetics in Church History

Truth demands confrontation; loving
confrontation, but confrontation nevertheless.
—FRANCIS SCHAEFFER[1]

As we mentioned briefly in the last chapter, modern apologetic efforts have largely been relegated to the work of philosophers and Christian thinkers who serve outside of the church. Of course, we realize that these individuals may also serve inside the

---

[1] Francis Schaeffer, *The Great Evangelical Disaster* (Wheaton, IL: Crossway, 1984), 64.

local church. For instance, famed Christian philosopher William Lane Craig has long taught a Sunday school class at his home church. However, we are trying to recover an ecclesial approach of apologetics where apologetic engagement and Christian philosophy is intertwined with the ministry of the local church and not completely detached from it.

This chapter will be largely descriptive in scope because we will briefly examine a mixture of historical figures who saw apologetics as a local ministry of the church. This chapter is not intended to be exhaustive or comprehensive in scope, but introductory. As we survey these individuals, we must remember that these Christian pastors lived in particular historical eras and contexts, so they engaged with specific beliefs, ideas, stories, and practices. Alongside our historical outline, another chapter goal is to highlight some of the contextual beliefs and practices within church history in order to demonstrate how we can learn from those apologetic approaches in our modern-day contexts. Thus, we are convinced that apologetics can guide and direct the church today into persuasive yet embodied ways of making Christ known.

Fast Facts: Tertullian's description of the Trinity in Latin (*tres personae, una substantia*) was one of the clearest explanations in the early church of the nature of the Triune God.

Early Apologetic Movements

One of the earliest Christian apologists was Justin Martyr (AD 100–165). A philosopher, Justin experienced an unexpected conversion to Christianity that led him on a lifelong pursuit of expressing the Christian faith in a manner that would appeal to thinking people. His most famous work, *Dialogue with Trypho*, presents a defense of the Christian faith. In his *First Apology* he makes the argument that all good and true philosophy is rooted in the writings of Moses.[2] In one sense, Martyr was the first Christian philosopher who worked in and alongside the local church but does not appear to have engaged in apologetics from the local church. This would fit what many today view as the work of the apologist. However, Martyr's apologetic argument is grounded in a commitment and defense of the gospel given to the church.

In *First Apology*, Martyr goes to great lengths to explain and defend the practices and doctrines of the church. Central to his defense of the church is a description of what the gospel produces among the people of the church:

> If we looked for a human kingdom, we should also deny our Christ. . . . We who formerly delighted in sexual sin, now embrace chastity alone; we who formerly used magical arts, dedicate ourselves to the good and only God; we who valued

---

[2] Justin Martyr, *First Apology*, 59.

above all things the acquisition of wealth and possessions, now bring what we have into a common stock, and share with everyone in need; we who hated and destroyed one another, and on account of their different manners would not live with men of a different tribe, now, since the coming of Christ, live in unity with them, and pray for our enemies, and endeavor to persuade those who hate us unjustly to live in conformity with the good precepts of Christ, to the end that they may become partakers with us of the same joyful hope of a reward from God the ruler of all.[3]

Defining Our Terms: Gnosticism (its adherents being known as gnostics) was a complex blend of various philosophies and dualistic spiritualities with Christian theology. This led to a range of heresies that denied the material nature of the incarnation, the belief in a distant and seemingly unknowable God, the inherent evil of the material world, and the need to seek and possess secret knowledge (gnosis) for one's spiritual progression.

In short, while Martyr is not a pastor acting as an apologist, his apologetic was primarily rooted in his commitment to and defense of the church, not just abstract propositional statements of truth.

---

[3] Martyr, 14.

Similar to Martyr is the life and work of Athenagoras (AD 133–190). A philosopher by training, he converted to Christianity and (possibly) became a teacher at an early Christian catechetical school. Regardless of his eventual vocation, what we know of Athenagoras is that he boldly defended the Christian faith from charges of atheism (a common charge, in the Roman world, against those who rejected Roman polytheism). What is striking is that Athenagoras supplied a robust defense of monotheism that is distinctly Christian. His goal was not to merely argue for the monotheistic worldview of the Christian faith, but to argue explicitly for Christian monotheism (something that would later be recognized as trinitarian monotheism). Both Martyr and Athenagoras were early Christian philosophers and apologists who defended the Christian faith. Both appear to have operated alongside the church rather than from the local church. However, this is the exception, not the rule, among the early Christians.

Irenaeus (AD 130–202) served as bishop for the church in Lyon as he sought to expand the church in what is now known as France. His great missionary zeal led to the expansion of the church in his region. His ministry was marked by leading the truth through both contention with the gnostics and enduring persecution from the pagans in Lyon. While we know that Irenaeus was an active writer, his surviving works are limited to just two. One of which, *Against Heresies*, is apologetic in nature. In *Against Heresies*, Irenaeus persuasively argues for Christian orthodoxy as he systematically dismantles the central claims of the gnostics. The work of Irenaeus was produced *for* the church and *from* the church. This church-centric pattern is what develops among early Christian thinkers. That is to say, it is common to find that the premier defenders of the Christian faith were more like Irenaeus than Martyr.

Perhaps the most prolific ante-Nicene trinitarian developments resulted from the works of Tertullian (AD 160–225). He is the first person to use the Latin word *trinitas* in describing the Godhead. Tertullian is a giant in the historical development of orthodoxy and Christian philosophy. Following his conversion to Christianity, Tertullian was ordained as an elder in the church in Carthage. Known as a fiery and unflinching debater, Tertullian addressed his most well-known work, *Apology*, to the Roman authorities. His defense of Christianity aimed to demonstrate the consistency of the Christian worldview, versus that of paganism, and to correct outlandish accusations made against churches. Additionally, Tertullian wrote against those who promulgated false doctrine. His *Prescription Against Heretics* was meant to correct false doctrine that was circulating in the name of Christianity. Although his intellect and comprehension of philosophy and rhetoric of his day matched that of Athenagoras and Martyr, Tertullian's apologetic was produced *for* the church and *from* the church.

To be clear, context matters. In the early church, there were no lavishly funded seminaries that equipped Christian thinkers to begin successful parachurch ministries (we are not sure any professor would say seminaries are lavishly funded today either). There was the church and only the church. Additionally, the cultural milieu in which the church was born quickly became hostile to the claims of Christianity. Thus, the church and only the local church could be the focus of ministerial work. Missionaries were sent from churches. Theologians and Christian writers operated primarily from churches.

This context still applies for much of the world today where Christianity is either illegal or at least looked upon with disdain. In the West, we enjoy an anomaly in which we have absolute freedom to employ methods that quite frankly are untenable in places such as North Korea or Iran. We are not arguing that had the early Christians enjoyed the same freedoms that we have that they would have elected to reject any kind of formalized Christian thinktank or parachurch ministry that focused on cultural engagement with the gospel. In fact, we are sure they would have developed something because they did eventually develop seminary-like apparatuses to equip thinkers for the work of the ministry. However, we are arguing that history demonstrates that one of the best ways to engage and navigate hostile cultural environments is to ground apologetic engagement under the oversight and auspices of the local church.

Medieval and Early Modern Apologetic Movements

Thomas Aquinas (AD 1225–1274) is perhaps one of the most influential Christian philosophers whose work transgresses denominational lines. You may ask, though, "Can Aquinas be categorized as a figure who fits into 'pastoral' apologetics?" Considering he carried the titles of friar and priest, we believe he is an excellent candidate.

Although Aquinas produced dozens of works, two significant ones are the *Summa contra gentiles* and the *Summa theologiae* (hereafter, *ST*). In *ST*, Aquinas divides his work into four parts: (1) the nature of God, (2) human action and its causes, (3) the philosophical and theological virtues, and (4) the sacraments. His intention of writing *ST* is largely about theological discipleship, but it has apologetic undertones. He is equipping pastors (and new believers) to think theologically and philosophically, which means this paradigm would have shaped their own ministries. As can be suspected from our outline of *ST*, Aquinas did not distinguish between ecclesial and academic apologetics—a more realistic gap later in the medieval era. For him, healthy evangelism, discipleship, and apologetics were done from within the boundaries of the Christian faith, not apart from it. As he had learned from both Augustine and Anselm, *fides quaerens intellectum* (faith seeks understanding), and we are convinced that such faith is grounded and generated from within local churches.

A general introduction to Western history will demonstrate a lull in Christian philosophy in the late medieval period from approximately 1300 to 1500. Yet we must not make the mistake in assuming that philosophy and theology were unrelated disciplines from the pre-Socratic to the medieval period. They were intricately intertwined for centuries. Thus, Protestant reformers such as Martin Luther and John Calvin would have received training in both areas via the subjects of grammar, rhetoric, logic, arithmetic, geometry, astronomy, and music. For Catholics, it was the Jesuits who helped retrieve and renew the spirit of the intellectual tradition during this period. In other words, no hard rifts existed between philosophy and theology for the German and French Reformers and the Jesuit order—which also meant no hard rifts existed between pastoral apologetics and academic apologetics.

For instance, Calvin wrote pastoral works, such as the *Institutes*, that were intended to equip pastors and laypersons in theological education; works like these were a familiar medium within the classical education of his day. Historically, the *Institutes* is considered one of the most powerful systematic and theological tomes of the Protestant faith, but it's rarely described as apologetic. Yet Scott Oliphant and William Edgar write, "Calvin the lawyer-theologian responded [to questions of theological orthodoxy] with [the *Institutes*] proving that the Reformed faith was indeed the historic Christian position."[4] Oliphant and Edgar add that Calvin began the *Institutes* "not with various attributes of God, or with the doctrine of Scripture, or even with 'my only comfort in life and in death,' but with the knowledge of God."[5] Calvin's theological enterprise, we could say, interwove the subjects of theology, epistemology (study of knowledge), ethics, and ministry. Underneath the

---

[4] Scott Oliphant and William Edgar, "Calvin the Apologist," Westminster Theological Seminary, October 23, 2017, https://faculty.wts.edu/posts/calvin-the-apologist/.

[5] Oliphant and Edgar.

systematic topics of sin, justification, sacraments, and the like, lay an apologetic, a defense for the good, true, and beautiful Christian faith. For Calvin, knowledge of the triune God and one's relationship to this God would mature into a practical demonstration and defense of his gospel.[6]

Contemporary Apologetic Movements

Moving forward several hundred years beyond Calvin, we arrive at the twentieth and twenty-first centuries. Undoubtedly, we have left out many key figures, but this chapter's task is to introduce you to exemplary Christian pastors who entangle pastoral ministry and apologetics. The last major pastoral figure we will briefly explore is Timothy Keller, former pastor at Redeemer Church in Manhattan.

It is evident from his preaching style and his voluminous library of authored books that Keller has attempted to retrieve the Christian intellectual tradition for apologetic purposes. Before his retirement from Redeemer Church, Keller consistently shepherded Redeemer to engage in the marketplace of ideas while himself interacting with leading minds in the unbelieving world. As a prolific author, two of his most influential apologetic books are *The Reason for God* and *Making Sense of God*.

---

[6] See Calvin, *Institutes*, 1.1. He commences his entire work: "Our wisdom . . . consists almost entirely of two parts: the knowledge of God and ourselves."

For example, Keller opens *Making Sense of God* with a story of how Redeemer Church has held weekly discussions for any persons "skeptical that there is a God or any supernatural reality."[7] He adds that a medley of sources are considered, such as "personal experience, philosophy, history, sociology, as well as religious texts—in order to compare systems of belief and to weigh how much sense they make in comparison with one another."[8] Keller's methodology is this: to assume a post-Christian vantage point where the epistemic default is that transcendent realities are nearly unimaginable. And working from within this perspective, he guides skeptical participants into making sense of their world with and without God. This apologetic model is difficult and requires patience and persistence. But it is an exemplary model of cultural apologetics because it works within secular frameworks in order to demonstrate the fractures of secularity and the cohesiveness of Christianity.

Additionally, Joshua Chatraw, who currently serves as Beeson Divinity School's Billy Graham Chair of Evangelism and Cultural Apologetics, previously moved his ministry of equipping to Raleigh, North Carolina, where he served as theologian-in-residence at Holy Trinity Anglican Church. It is from this post that he directed the Center for Public Christianity, a nine-month training program

---

[7] Timothy Keller, *Making Sense of God: An Invitation to the Skeptical* (New York: Penguin Random House, 2016), 1.

[8] Keller, 1.

meant to equip Christians to engage in the marketplace of ideas. One of their central goals was to "equip leaders for the local church, partnering with churches across Raleigh to serve them and their missions."[9] This recentering of the apologetic enterprise to the oversight and function of the local church is a reclaiming of the pattern and practice of the early church and, we would argue, most closely embodies what the New Testament envisioned for the defense of the Christian faith.

I (Michael) have a good friend, Andy Brown, who serves as the pastor at First Baptist Church in Starkville, Mississippi. Similar to the paradigms as Keller and Chatraw, Andy has initiated the Starkville Institute to cultivate theological education from within the church. The Institute consists of three ten-week core seminars that rotate around three areas: Christian Scripture, Christian teaching, and Christian community. They even offer a two-year residency program intended to deepen students in Christian doctrine and practice. In many respects, the Institute is an ecclesial retrieval of theological formation of the church, and their hope is to generate a robust and holistic model for other local churches to adopt and contextualize.[10]

---

[9] See the Center for Public Christianity's website at https://centerfor publicchristianity.org/about.

[10] For more information about Starkville Institute and its discipleship model, see https://fbcstarkville.com/institute.

Conclusion

In our cultural context, an abundance of apologetic ministries abound—some tethered to churches while others are more properly called parachurch ministries. Being a parachurch apologetics ministry has its advantages. For instance, by not affiliating with a specific church or denomination, the ministry will have greater access to equip or partner with churches across denominational lines. We completely understand this advantage. However, we do not believe this is a carte-blanche warrant for the independent existence of such ministries.

Many of these ministries have produced some good fruit that has blessed the body of Christ. Still, this fruit could and would be produced by similar efforts grounded in the ministry of the local church. Furthermore, our overall aim is to show that better fruit would be produced by grounding apologetics in the context of the local church.

In Ephesians 4, the apostle Paul describes the gifts that Christ has given to the church for her equipping:

> And he (**Christ**) himself gave some to be apostles, some prophets, some evangelists (**This is not the same thing as being an apologist; see our following commentary.**), some pastors and teachers (**This could and perhaps should be understood as pastor-teacher, since the office of elder necessitates the ability to rightly divide the Scriptures.**),

to equip the saints **(believers)** for the work of ministry **(Elsewhere Paul describes this work as the ministry of rec- onciliation.),** to build up the body of Christ **(The church, which in the context of Paul's letter is clearly local in focus even if it is universal in application. Paul's understanding of the church is a universal church that is comprised of local churches. Given the nature of Paul's letters, he does not speak of a generic "church" as we often do in modern vernacular. Instead, he envisions the universal church being the totality of local churches.),** until we all **(mem- bers of the local church and the local churches, plural)** reach unity in the faith and in the knowledge of God's Son, growing into maturity with a stature measured by Christ's fullness. (Eph 4:11–13)[11]

These individuals that Paul describes as being given by Christ are given to the local church. Each of these individual giftings and accompanying roles exist for the purpose of building up the local church, which collectively makes up the universal body of Christ. Nowhere in the list can you find apologist as a gifting or call- ing from Christ. Some could argue that an evangelist is a type of apologist. We slightly disagree. In fact, the church health ministry 9Marks has succinctly enumerated the difference between apolo- getics and evangelism:

---

[11] Our comments and clarifications are emboldened for the reader.

- **Difference 1:** Evangelism is telling others the gospel. Apologetics is defending the truth of the Christian faith.

- **Difference 2:** Apologetics addresses everything from the existence of God to the reliability of the Old and New Testaments. In contrast, evangelism is telling one specific message: the good news about what Jesus Christ has done in order to save sinners.

- **Difference 3:** Another difference between apologetics and evangelism is that apologetics usually requires some level of intellectual sophistication. Apologetics can involve logical arguments, historical debates, philosophical discussions, interpretive disputes, and more. On the other hand, evangelism is simply telling others the message about Jesus Christ. That's something every Christian—even a brand-new Christian—should be able to do.[12]

Moreover, most operating definitions employed by those who would be seen as professional apologists make similar distinctions. Seminaries offer degrees in evangelism or degrees in apologetics, while others provide a degree in apologetics and evangelism. The near consensus in the apologetics world is that while evangelism

---

[12] 9Marks, "What Is the Relationship between Apologetics and Evangelism?," 9Marks, accessed January 31, 2023, https://www.9marks.org/answer/what-relationship-between-apologetics-and-evangelism/.

and apologetics can and should be related to one another, they are distinctly different activities.[13]

Now, let's return to the issue of credibility mentioned earlier in this chapter. The Scriptures have clear and serious character qualifications for those who serve in the office of elder or pastor. While not every individual listed in Ephesians 4 is described as an elder, the context would seem to imply that an equal level of seriousness would be given to the role with which these individuals serve the local church. Therefore, most of the character qualifications of pastors should also apply to those holding the other positions described by Paul.

In the age of podcasts, vlogs, blogs, Twitter, and YouTube, anyone with a philosopher's mind can dub themselves an apologist and begin to defend and represent the Christian faith to the unbelieving world. They can do so in a way that seems authoritative even when it is not. Because we have divorced the apologetic endeavor from the only institution to which it is tied in Scripture (the local church) we have lone-ranger apologists, who have not been vetted on character or theological acumen, speaking as if they are the defenders of the faith. When an individual takes it upon him- or herself to be the defender or arbiter of orthodoxy and the discerner

---

[13] A very helpful resource that demonstrates a faithful expression of evangelistic and apologetic engagement within an increasingly anti-Christian culture is Elliot Clark, *Evangelism as Exiles: Life on Mission as Strangers in Our Own Land* (Bannockburn, IL: The Gospel Coalition, 2019).

of truth, who holds them accountable? Time and time again, we have witnessed this become a credibility issue among unbelievers and believers alike.[14]

Returning then to the words of the apostle Paul, we find evangelists given to the local church (those with a unique boldness and ability to clearly communicate the gospel to unbelievers), but we do not find apologists. However, going back to chapter 1, we argued that an apologetic mandate is given specifically to pastors and in general to all believers. Thus, it would make sense that the pastor-teacher described by Paul in Ephesians 4 would act as a defender of the faith while also equipping (again, as described by Paul) the body of Christ to defend the faith. Regardless of how we spin the language, we cannot find the office or calling of apologist apart from the specific role of pastor in the local church or in general an apologetic mandate that applies to all Christians.

Additionally, it should be noted that in our model individuals are accountable to one another as they seek to demonstrate and defend the gospel together. The local church becomes the cultivator

---

[14] We could list numerous examples of this phenomenon. We have consciously chosen to not publicly list those names so that we do not inadvertently slip into the sin of slander. Moreover, we're aware of two professional apologists, operating ministries independent of local church oversight, that have engaged in moral failings. Both individuals were only sidelined from their public activity for a very brief period. This has been noted by unbelievers as an example of the "sham" that Christian truth claims must be. We have a credibility issue.

of Christly character and the incubator of apologetics, and we are convinced that these two should work hand in hand. To connect this conversation with Paul's body metaphor in 1 Corinthians 12, Christ unites the body for a diversity of apologetic tasks. Richard Lints writes, "Our identities are shaped by those around us even as we also influence the identities of those around us."[15] Even though the church can be unified under a specific vision of apologetics, how individual members incarnate that vision may be complex and diverse. For instance, in a multiethnic church, answering specific questions and defending the gospel in an Asian community may be drastically different from answering certain questions and defending the gospel in a predominantly Hispanic community. Yet each community has the same goal: to give a reasonable yet persuasive defense of the gospel.

Our genuine hope is to recapture this pastoral vision outlined by Paul in Ephesians 4, where the pastor-teacher acts and models what it means to defend the faith while also equipping the body of Christ to defend the faith. In this chapter, we have outlined numerous pastoral figures and their models of apologetic ministry throughout Christian history to exhibit that our pastor-as-apologist model is a both a biblical and ancient one. It is not novel. Without these exemplars, our argument is moot. As we see it, when we retrieve

---

[15] Richard Lints, *Uncommon Unity: Wisdom for the Church in an Age of Division* (Bellingham, WA: Lexham, 2022), 107.

this biblical and ancient paradigm of pastor-apologist, we are able to recover an intellectual tradition that winsomely and contextually defends the excellencies of Christ's gospel.

Heart Work (Reflection Questions)

1. In what way is your church emulating the from-the-church and for-the-church apologetic activity of the early church?

2. What action steps can you take right now to better prepare your church to engage in the apologetic endeavor from the church and for the church?

3. Where do you see the most potential for your congregation to demonstrate, defend, and proclaim the central truth claims of the gospel to your unbelieving neighbors?

Chapter 3

A Practical Handbook for Preaching Apologetics

We have talked about the manner and mode of preaching,
but contextualization also has much to do with the
content. A sermon should be unengaging to a person
because, though expressing accurate biblical truth, it
does not connect biblical teaching to the main objections
and questions people in that culture have about faith.
—TIMOTHY KELLER[1]

---

[1] Timothy Keller, *Center Church: Doing Balanced, Gospel-Centered Ministry in Your City* (Grand Rapids: Zondervan, 2012), 95.

For pastors desiring to incorporate apologetic elements into their teaching but unsure where to start, our aim in this chapter is to provide some theological and practical guidance. Theologically, we will summarize academic elements of various apologetic issues, such as the problem of evil, the cosmological argument, the probability of Jesus's resurrection, and the reliability of the Bible. We mention these particular topics because of their prevalence in Western (and specifically American) culture. It is worth pointing out that each of these topics has an underlying theme: skepticism. From the problem of evil to the reliability of the Bible, everyday Americans question, doubt, and wrestle with the existence of God, the likelihood of the resurrection of a Jewish man, and the trustworthiness of the Bible. If doubt is the epistemic default of the American imagination, how do we craft sermons and develop lessons to meet people where they are at?

Practically, we would like to help the pastor incorporate gentle yet strong defenses of the faith into weekly sermons and other teaching environments. Learning how and when to blend apologetic responses for sincere doubts is difficult but not impossible. This chapter functions like a practical handbook in order to affirm the complexity of doubts while intentionally priming and provoking skeptics toward an openness to Christian belief.

The Problem of Evil: Academic Engagement

One of the most popular and effective arguments against the existence of God is the presence of pain, suffering, and evil in the world. This objection is effective in raising doubts for the believer while enabling the skeptic to remain comfortable in his or her skepticism. Because the problem of evil is an influential argument, we will spend more time interacting with it than most others in the chapter.[2] The difficulty in responding to this objection is not due to its strength as an argument against Christianity; rather, its strength lies in the emotional response it conjures.[3] Sadly, the emotion-evoking rhetoric of the New Atheists tends to blur the lines between what makes sense logically and what speaks to the heart emotionally.

Bios in Brief: Sam Harris, Richard Dawkins, Christopher Hitchens, and Daniel Dennett (collectively sometimes referred to as the four horsemen) are generally considered the chief thinkers of New Atheism.

---

[2] This section originally appeared as a published paper: Dayton Hartman, "A Presuppositional Response to the Problem of Evil," *Journal of the International Society of Christian Apologetics* 5, no. 1 (2012): 31–45.

[3] A prime example of this is the manner in which New Atheist Sam Harris addresses the existence of evil and suffering in the world.

Addressing the problem of evil is made more difficult because those defending Christian theism may fall prey to the intended use of this objection, which is detachment from logic and submersion into emotion. Therefore, rather than debate specific elements of evil that plague the world from the outset, perhaps another course could be more fruitful and far less entangling.

This new course is this: to raise the problem of evil in a manner consistent with their own worldview. We must first illustrate a big picture prior to the engagement of any particulars of evil. This route will get to the heart of the issue being questioned. That question is simply this: "Evil clearly exists, so which worldview provides the best explanation and solution for the problem of evil?" Requiring skeptics to remain consistent with their own worldview in answering this crucial question will prove most effective in accomplishing the apologetic task.

Perhaps the most basic of all the classic statements regarding the problem of evil are as follows:

1. If God were all-powerful, he would be able to prevent or destroy all evil.
2. If God were all-good, he would desire to prevent or to destroy all evil.
3. Evil exists.
4. Therefore, an all-powerful, all-good God does not exist.[4]

---

[4] Adapted from John Frame, *Apologetics to the Glory of God* (Phillipsburg, NJ: P&R, 1994), 150.

William Rowe formulates the problem this way:

1. There exist instances of intense suffering which an omnip-
    otent, omniscient being could have prevented without
    thereby losing some greater good or permitting some evil
    equally bad or worse.
2. An omniscient, wholly good being would prevent the
    occurrence of any intense suffering it could, unless it could
    not do so without thereby losing some great good or per-
    mitting some evil equally bad or worse.

Given the conditions he observes in the world, Rowe concludes,

3. There does not exist an omnipotent, omniscient, wholly
    good being.[5]

The traditional formulation of the problem assumes a few critical
facts: First, what can be objectively identified as evil exists. Certainly,
the use of the term *objectively* could be debated.[6] Still, this concept
is being assumed to furnish a viable premise on which to deny the

---

[5] William Rowe, "The Inductive Argument from Evil Against the
Existence of God," in *Philosophy of Religion*, ed. Louis P. Pojman (Albany,
NY: Wadsworth, 1998), 212.

[6] Paul Gould offers some concise definitions of objective and subjective realities: "Subjectivism is the view that *all* moral values and obligations
are grounded in individual beliefs or preferences. *Objectivism* is the view
that at least some moral values and obligations are independent of minds
or speakers." Gould, *A Good and True Story: Eleven Clues to Understanding
Our Universe and Your Place in It* (Grand Rapids: Brazos, 2022), 91. We will
adopt Gould's categories throughout the remainder of this chapter.

existence of God. Second, God would want to, and actually would, destroy all evil. Third, the reality we experience is therefore logically incoherent with Christian theism. The first and third assumptions directly demonstrate worldview inconsistency.

The Problem of Evil, the Role of Logic, and Worldview

It is interesting that atheism is purported to be a position that is logical and consistent with reality. Given the materialist worldview of atheism, its use of and insistence on logic is highly problematic. In an attempt to circumvent the problems surrounding their use of logic, atheists have presented a few options for explaining the origin and authority of logic. A manner in which atheists attempt to explain logic is by claiming that logic comes from nature. That is to say that logic merely describes what we observe in nature.

The problem with this explanation is that it assumes logic. The way in which occurrences in nature are classified is through the use of the scientific method. However, this is circular reasoning. The scientific method is a viable method by which to assess occurrences in nature chiefly because it assumes that logic exists. Classification of what is observed in nature occurs through the use of logic. Scientists do not derive logic from nature and then define what they observe in nature by what they have derived. No, they assume that what occurs does so in a manner that is logical.

Another popular proposal for the existence of logic is its development as a means for survival. This proposal fails on a few accounts. First, this assumes that an impersonal process can produce what is personal. Second, this assumes that adherence to logic assures survival. Experience proves that this is simply not true. It would seem as if species that do not possess capabilities for recognizing logic appear to have a greater ability for survival than beings that recognize logic.[7] Third, proposing that evolution explains the origin of logic is also circular because it would demand that evolutionary processes would exhibit the use of the laws of logic. It would seem as if evolutionary processes logically recognize that logic is necessary for survival. Thus, this option for explaining logic raises more questions than it answers.

Some atheists explain that the laws of logic are little more than generally agreed-upon principles. Yet logic transcends the groups for which they are normatively considered as conventions (i.e., Western civilization). If logic is formed by an informal vote or consensus, then the pervasive nature of these laws in human experience is unexplainable.

These inconsistencies can be further demonstrated by using the Transcendental Argument for God (henceforth, TAG).[8] This

---

[7] Frame, *Apologetics to the Glory of God*, 104.

[8] TAG could be best understood as a family of arguments rather than a single argument. There is no definitive manner in which to state the argument, and it can be adapted to the audience's understanding of logic.

argument is premised on recognizable constants used in logic. These constants or absolutes are generally referred to as the "laws of logic". These laws are the law of identity,[9] the law of non-contradiction,[10] and the law of excluded middle.[11]

The laws of logic are constant and consistent throughout human experience. For example, the laws of logic demand that there is no such thing as a square-circle. Similarly, the laws of logic preclude the possibility that we may one day discover a marauding band of married bachelors. The laws of logic must be true at all times. If these laws were not true, then the aforementioned impossibilities would become potential realities. Any attempt to prove that these laws are not absolutely true would be self-defeating, for in demonstrating that these laws are not universally binding, one must use said laws in presenting one's case. Additionally, without the existence of the laws of logic, rational exchanges would be utterly impossible. The exchange of information would be, at best, subjective and, at worst, absurd. Therefore, objecting to the absolute nature of the laws of logic is a futile exercise.

Building on this understanding of logic, TAG proposes that the laws of logic are transcendent. This characteristic means that

---

[9] Something is what it is and is not what it is not. For instance, a human is a human and not also a dog.

[10] Something cannot be both true and false at the same time in the same way.

[11] A given statement is either true or false. For example, you are reading *The Pastor as Apologist*. That is either a true or false statement.

regardless of time, location, or the existence of humans, the laws remain true. To deny such a proposal would be to allow, at some point, that what is logical could change. In other words, there may be a time in the future when square-circles come into existence or when married bachelors become a recognized minority population.

The transcendence of logic can further be confirmed by the fact that the laws of logic are recognized by different persons from different contexts at different times. Human beings often differ on tastes in music, ice cream, and the best places to vacation. Yet logic supersedes these subjective nuances of human opinion and thinking and is therefore different from and not dependent on the thoughts of humans. Rather, logic transcends human thinking and is recognized or discovered by humans.

Another aspect of logic is its immaterial and conceptual nature. Logic has no mass or material composition. Logic is not produced by any physical process within the universe and is not dependent on any continuing process for its existence. While these logical absolutes are not composed of matter, they are recognized and considered by human minds. However, these absolutes are not created by human minds. To be created by a human mind would render them subjective. Yet that which is conceptual is produced by a mind. Given the conceptual and absolute nature of logic, it must be the product of an infinite, non-human mind. Within the bounds of Christian theism, this mind is recognized as the mind of God. This is not to say that God created logic. Rather, logic emanates from the mind of God. God is logical, therefore all that he creates accords from the logical processes of his mind.

By stating the problem of evil in a logical manner, the skeptic assumes specific properties within his universe that simply cannot exist. Given the presuppositions of atheism, it would be impossible to demonstrate that evil exists and that this is a problem for theism. Still, the existence of evil is in fact an issue that must be addressed by theists because a logical argument for the non-existence of God can be made based on the existence of evil.

Still, this argument is only logical in a universe foreign to an atheistic worldview. Proposing that the existence of evil is a logical problem (meaning that it requires attention) for Christian theism is a self-defeating statement. If Christian theism is false, then Rowe's syllogism on the problem of evil stated above is, at best, subjective reasoning; at worst, it is utterly meaningless. Both the atheist and theist can, and should, agree that the problem of evil is not subjective or absurd.

To summarize, the topic of the problem of evil cannot be examined by itself—in a vacuum, so to speak. Rather, it must be entertained within one's larger worldview in order to discover its weaknesses and strengths.

At this point, we will move the discussion forward to consider tangible examples of evil. In so doing, we turn our focus to our everyday world to discern how one worldview may better acknowledge, interpret, and explain evil.

Making Sense of Evil in Our Everyday World

Atheists rightly observe the immense pain, suffering, and injustice in the world and deem it evil or morally repugnant. So when atheists proclaim the evil of rape, murder, and thievery, theists can agree. But only from a theistic worldview can someone observe all that takes place in the world and deem it genuinely evil in any meaningful, objective sense. As mentioned in the previous section, any statement declaring some action or activity "evil" assumes some standard by which good and evil can be judged.

This is problematic because atheism tends to reduce morals to either personal preferences or to cultural constructs. The former has its modern origins in David Hume, who connects ethics to human reason and desires.[12] Following many of the central arguments first outlined by Thomas Hobbes, Hume's aim was to develop a virtuous atheism.[13] Without a theistic God in his worldview, Hume had to establish how humanity produces moral choices, so he claimed

---

[12] See David Hume, *A Treatise of Human Nature*, ed. L. A. Selby-Bigge, 2nd ed. (Oxford: Clarendon, 1975).

[13] To be clear, Hume doesn't seem to arrogantly suggest that religion is always destructive of morality; rather, Hume's attempt is to articulate an autonomous, secular morality without God in the equation. Like many of his predecessors and contemporaries, Hume tries to explore novel arenas of philosophy without the expected conversation partners of theism. Autonomy (from the theistic religions) was, undoubtedly, one of the philosophical principles and experiments of most of modernity's figures.

that morality originates in the psyche and the passions, thus making ethical living fundamentally a matter of personal preferences.[14] Hume proposes that morality is not merely a subjective, in-the-eyes-of-the-beholder way of life; rather, human reason becomes the autonomous arbiter of a society's common good, and humans should submit their passions and inclinations to reason's guidance.

The latter example has had advocates since ancient Greece, as in the philosophy of Protagoras, who notably quipped, "Man is the measure of all things." In short, human beings are the constructors of what is good, beautiful, and true.[15] To state it differently, human beings create social worlds such as religion, politics, and ethics. Following Plato's and Aristotle's assessment of Protagoras's claim, it seems Protagoras suggested that all human knowledge and even value judgments are derivative of human sensations. The reader may see similarities between Hume and Protagoras, so let's clarify Protagoras's larger point: Humans know their world via their senses, yet societies are erected, established, and legislated by a smaller body of humans who decide what is good, bad, and ugly, making things, such as morality, a social construct.

Whether we are talking about morals as a personal preference or a cultural construct, a blatant fact remains: Morals are entirely

---

[14] See Hume, *A Treatise of Human Nature*.

[15] As many Protagoras scholars have noted, his maxim is undoubtedly, and possibly intentionally, ambiguous. Two of the primary sources we have of Protagoras and what he meant derive from Plato and Aristotle, so we could admit that our access to Protagoras is already reconstructed.

subjective in both categories. Commenting on this bleak situation, Winfried Corduan writes, "Without a God behind the world, suffering and evil can be no more than painful indicators of the futility of a meaningless life."[16] A century before Corduan, Richard Bentley claimed in his Boyle lecture:

> And if atheism should . . . become universal in this nation . . . [then] farewell all ties of friendship and principles of honor; all love for our country and loyalty to our prince; nay, farewell all government and society itself, all professions and arts, and conveniences of life, all that is laudable or valuable in the world.[17]

Corduan's and Bentley's comments have interesting effects. If all morality is ultimately subjective and rooted in finite structures (whether individually or collectively), then nothing can be deemed truly good or evil, such as social issues pertaining to human rights and the value of life. As Greg Koukl and Francis Beckwith point out, "The notions of human respect and dignity depend on the existence of moral truth."[18] If one removes the objectivity of truth and the binding nature of logic, then the only conclusion one can

---

[16] Winfried Corduan, *No Doubt About It* (Nashville: B&H Academic, 1997), 128.

[17] Richard Bentley, "Folly of Atheism," in *The Works of Richard Bentley* (New York: AMS, 1966), 25.

[18] Gregory Koukl and Francis Beckwith, *Relativism: Feet Firmly Planted in Mid-Air* (Grand Rapids: Baker, 1998), 21.

arrive at is that "nothing has transcendent value, including human beings."[19] Our claim is that worldviews matter and, more importantly, a coherency within worldviews matters.

Christian apologists like Francis Schaeffer demonstrated that strong, consistent, and coherent worldviews were the ones that best described reality. Schaeffer even advocated for an apologetic paradigm where unbelievers begin with the external world and what humanity itself is and then let those persons draw out the implications of their worldview to show their real need for God.[20] Schaeffer writes that the skeptic undergoes this experience "so that he may realize his system has no answer to the crucial questions of life," like the problem of evil.[21]

When atheists object to the existence of God based on the existence of evil, apologists must respond by addressing these false assumptions. Certainly, evil exists; that is not in dispute. However, the recognition of evil from the atheistic perspective is in dispute. The reason for this disputation arises from the fact that, in order to object to God's existence based on the existence of evil, one must assume a degree of objectivity in proclaiming that what is undesirable

---

[19] Koul and Beckwith, 22.

[20] Schaeffer called this paradigm "taking the roof off." Using a house metaphor in relation to worldviews, he illustrated that a construction of beliefs was like building a home. Some (philosophical) homes are built on weak foundations with weak walls and dilapidating roofs, whereas others are strong and well-built to sustain the tempests of reality. See Francis Schaeffer, *The God Who Is There* (Downers Grove, IL: InterVarsity, 1998), 155–58.

[21] Schaeffer, 156.

is actually evil. The issue at hand is primarily this: Can anything be described as objectively, morally evil from the materialist perspective?

Following Corduan's and Bentley's concerns intertwined with Schaeffer's paradigm, it seems that moral absolutes, such as evil, need a worldview that includes immaterial, transcendent realities, which the materialist worldview cannot account for.

Pointing out this dilemma, philosopher Chad Meister writes, "One cannot consistently affirm both that there are no objective moral values, on the one hand, and that rape, torture and the like are objectively morally evil on the other."[22] Clearly, nothing can be called objectively good or evil unless transcultural, objective moral values by which we assess moral particulars actually exist. Given the "matter only" claims of atheism, immaterial, binding laws that provide the framework for moral decisions and assessment simply cannot exist. The only genuine out for the atheist is to claim that when a culture comes to a consensus about evil, that action or condition is actually evil. Taking this position raises a serious problem—namely, that "might makes right." The will of the masses dictates what can be called good or evil. Therefore, the actions of a given people could never be objectively deemed as immoral. So devastating events such as the Holocaust were little more than the cultural outworking of the consensus of a people group and cannot be objectively identified as immoral, grotesque, and haunting.

---

[22] William Lane Craig and Chad Meister, eds., *God Is Good, God Is Great* (Downers Grove, IL: InterVarsity, 2009), 109.

A problem further resides in the assumption that a cultural consensus may identify that which is good or evil apart from objective moral values. How does one assess what constitutes a cultural consensus for the definition of good or evil? Is it a simple statistical majority or is it a two-thirds majority? What statistical requirement could be deemed as the moral or good rule to which all cultures should adhere?

Additionally, how does one define cultural consensus when even the very definition of a culture or people group could be questioned? For instance, it is recognized that within every nation exist subcultures. At what point should it be considered morally good to allow subcultures to dictate for themselves what is good or evil? What are the criteria for adjudicating between these subcultures? How could anyone objectively identify the activities of a subculture of necrophiliacs as genuinely evil in such a world? The answer is clear: It would be impossible apart from moral tyranny (which would be logically permissible).

Furthermore, individuals do not live in the real world in such a manner as to remain consistent with this subjective moral proposition. If morals were simply cultural constructs, when the skeptic hears news of genocide or ritualistic mutilation of female reproductive organs, they would not respond with, "That is evil!" No! Instead, they would reply with, "Well, that is not my moral taste, but to each his own." Yet time and time again the leaders of modern atheism exclaim in horror at the atrocities carried out around the

Notable Quotes: "It looks like our world derives not only its *being* from some kind of transcendent foundation but also a kind of intricate *meaning* from it as well—much like a story derives meaning from an author. For in our world we discover truths (like math) and beauty (like music) that seem out of place within a strictly naturalistic conception of reality. Moreover, most of us live on the assumption of certain values (like love) and intuitions (like rationality) that are difficult to substantiate within the boundaries of pure naturalism. Where do these alluringly metaphysical qualities come from? Better sense can be made out of our world, and of our experience within it, on the hypothesis that it has been ordered or structured by something ulterior to itself. . . . Consider that the universe includes *us*—people who reason and love, who feel and imagine, who create and dream, who thirst for meaning and happiness. It's strange to think that the effect should be greater than the cause—that the personal should derive from the impersonal, that a universe devoid of meaning should produce creatures who cannot live without it."

Gavin Ortlund, *Why God Makes Sense in a World That Doesn't* (Grand Rapids: Baker Academic, 2021), 111–12.

world. This is especially true when atheists believe that they or their interests have been wronged.

As C. S. Lewis has pointed out, even those who deny the objectivity or absolute nature of the law of nature (moral absolutes) assume these absolutes when they themselves or their interests are wronged. This sentiment goes beyond frustration with some outside force infringing on their preference or happiness. What does occur is a negative reaction at the thought that those harming the atheist or their interests violated some standard the atheist assumes to be binding, and that should be obvious to the outside agent.[23]

It is one thing to assert that an action, situation, or condition is evil; it is an entirely different issue to justify one's belief that an action, situation, or condition is evil. Only by assuming the very same conditions they are denying (objective, transcendent moral values) can a skeptic make any definitive moral judgment.

The Problem of Evil: Conclusion

Apologetic engagement must insist that the skeptic remain consistent to their worldview when approaching the problem

---

[23] C. S. Lewis, *The Complete C. S. Lewis Signature Classics* (New York: HarperOne, 2007), 15. Lewis goes on to argue that despite varying cultural interpretation of the Law of Nature, it is nevertheless universal. So while some may argue that a man can only have one wife and another argues he may have many wives, both assume that it would be absolutely wrong to take any woman a man pleases. This is especially true if that woman (via a marriage covenant) "belongs" to the man from whom she is taken.

of evil. Why? Because such individuals consistently live within the bounds of their worldview presuppositions. Very few atheists actually take their presuppositions (that logic is not absolute and that morals are subjective) to their logical extreme. However, as John Frame observes, "The unbeliever may resist this extreme [the logical conclusion of his presuppositions], for he knows it is implausible, but there is nothing in his adopted philosophy to guard against it."[24]

When it comes to the problem of evil, atheists must ultimately borrow from a theistic worldview to deny theism. First, the atheist must assume the existence and authority of logic. While the atheistic worldview does not allow for immaterial, transcendent laws, the atheist must assume as much to argue against the existence of God. Second, the atheist must propose that the world is filled with what could be objectively called evil or things that ought not be. The atheistic worldview does not allow such an assessment. So in order to raise the issue of evil as an objection to the existence of God, the atheist must once again borrow from a theistic worldview. Inconsistency is the tell-tale sign of a failed argument. Therefore, it behooves the Christian apologist to demonstrate this inconsistency and to demand the atheist to account for his or her borrowing from a worldview in order to deny it.[25]

---

[24] Frame, *Apologetics to the Glory of God*, 194.
[25] See Bahnsen, *Pushing the Antithesis*, 105.

The Problem of Evil: Sermon Starter

When the problem of pain, evil, or suffering arises in the text of Scripture, pastors should acknowledge the problem. Speak to the issues of pain and suffering in the world and in the room. Reassure those in your congregation that when suffering hits and when evil takes its toll, it is natural to question God. Reinforce to your congregation that God does not fear their questions, but we cannot attack God with our accusations.

I (Dayton) like to remind people that the reason why death feels wrong is because it is wrong. The reason why suffering feels wrong is because it is wrong. Our sense of the wrongness of pain, evil, and suffering is because we innately know that human beings have dignity and value. Our visceral reaction to pain and suffering in the world, whether from a believer or skeptic, is always grounded in a desire for someone outside of ourselves to make things right. These are the aches of the human heart for redemption.

Reassure Christians who have doubts because of pain that their doubts reinforce the fact that God is present, and he created us for a different kind of world than the one we live in right now. If there were no God, pain and suffering would not cause us to question him. Our response to the presence of pain, evil, and suffering would not be all that different from our response to the changing of time or watching a plant wilt in the heat of the day. We would simply recognize it is an inescapable and ultimately meaningless reality.

If you choose to use the TAG argument in your sermon as you address objections to God resulting from the problem of evil, pain, and suffering, keep the use brief and simple, and present the propositions on a screen if possible.

Tell the congregation that you are going to point out things they already know but maybe have not thought about. Assure them that they think philosophically every day, they just do not call it philosophy or logic.

Above all, have a tender heart as you address the problem of evil, pain, and suffering. No matter how self-defeating the objections to the existence of God or the truth of the Bible are based on the problem of evil, pain is still real. And while logical arguments can provide assurance, they do not heal hearts or bodies. Speak these arguments as invitations to the skeptic and as a soothing balm to the hearts of the aching Christian.

The Beginning: Why Things Exist

One of the strongest pieces of evidence for the existence of God is the universe itself. Why is there anything instead of nothing? Philosophers have sought to answer this question for centuries, and atheistic philosophers must engage in linguistic gymnastics to avoid the blunt reality that they have no compelling answer. Once we accept acknowledge that the existence of the universe necessitates an explanation, Christian philosophers will often point to the complexity of the universe, the necessary conditions for life, and irreducible complexity necessary for any and all life to exist. This classification of argumentation falls under the category of teleology.

However, I (Dayton) believe that requiring an explanation for the very existence of any and all things to be compelling evidence for the existence of God. One of the best examples of an argument from existence is the Kalām Cosmological Argument. Popularized by William Lane Craig, the argument is rooted in Islamic philosophy. It is not, however, an argument for the existence of the god of Islam as much as it is an argument for the existence of the god of bare monotheism.

William Lane Craig and the Kalām Cosmological Argument

The general argument, as presented by Craig, is this:

> Proposition One: Whatever begins to exist has a cause.
> Proposition Two: The universe began to exist.
> Conclusion: Therefore, the universe has a cause.

This seems obvious; however, it does require further explanation. First, everything observed by science as coming into existence has a clear cause for its existence. Things do not simply materialize. Second, the universe did come into existence, but the limitations of scientific inquiry can only be to research or develop models that attempt to explain what happened in the moments following the birth of the universe. This necessitates that something beyond the

> **Defining Our Terms:** Teleological arguments center around the evidences for an intelligent designer. Rather than relying primarily on philosophy, although philosophical elements are present in these arguments, teleology demonstrates an apparent design or purpose to various aspects of the universe and complex life.

material universe acted in a way to cause the material universe to come into existence. The logical explanation for this cause must be a being beyond our comprehension, not bound by the scientific laws that govern the material universe. Christians would say that this "uncaused, cause" is the God of the Scripture.

The only true escape for the skeptic would be if the material universe could be demonstrated to be eternal. However, this would only be an apparent escape from the conclusion that God exists rather than an actual escape. Why? In order for the universe to be eternal, there must be an infinite regression of events—which is logically impossible.

An actual infinite cannot exist in a real and material sense. The most helpful illustration I (Dayton) have found for this has been popularized by Craig and is known as Hilbert's Hotel.[26] The

---

[26] I explored this illustration by framing it as an apologetic against the claim of infinite god regression by Church of Jesus Christ of Latter-day Saints apologists. What is listed here is largely a direct quotation of that

premise of Hilbert's Hotel is that there exists a hotel that contains an infinite number of rooms for an infinite number of guests. This well-known illustration is historically argued as follows: Upon arriving at Hilbert's Hotel, guests find an infinite number of rooms; thus, a new guest seeking a room is informed that all of these rooms are in fact full because the infinite number of rooms are currently occupied by an infinite number of guests.[27] But the clerk is most accommodating and asks that all guests shift over by one room, thereby freeing one room for this new guest.[28] Because the number of rooms is infinite, it becomes possible to shift every person filling these rooms and there will still be more rooms.[29]

As Craig points out, the strange thing about this illustration is that such a process of accommodation could be repeated for an infinite number of guests and yet the hotel would never gain any more guests (in terms of total numbers) than were present upon the arrival of the first guest mentioned.[30] Stranger still is the fact that even if guests leave the hotel, all of the rooms remain full because

---

explanation from my book: Hartman, *Joseph Smith's Tritheism* (Eugene, OR: Wipf & Stock, 2014), 124–25.

[27] William Lane Craig, *The Kalām Cosmological Argument* (Eugene, OR: Wipf & Stock, 1979), 26.

[28] Craig; Graham Oppy, *Philosophical Perspectives on Infinity* (Cambridge: Cambridge University, 2009), 8–9.

[29] Michael Clark, *Paradoxes from A to Z*, 3rd ed. (London: Routledge, 2012), 94; Peter Higgins, *Numbers: A Very Short Introduction* (Oxford: Oxford University, 2011), 85–86.

[30] Craig, *The Kalām Cosmological Argument*, 27–28.

of the infinite number of guests occupying the infinite number of rooms.[31] In short, Hilbert's Hotel can in one instant have empty rooms yet be entirely full! It is an absurdity. This demonstrates that an infinite regression of aggregative finite structures cannot exist in a material universe.[32]

Just as the preceding illustration indicates the absurdity of an actual infinite, so does the reality of the present. Every human being will readily agree that they exist in the present. However, if an actual infinite regression of time and events is true, then the present could never have become a reality. The logic behind this proposition is simple: One could never span the successive and infinite series of events that preceded today. As J. P. Moreland has noted, if an individual attempts to span an infinite number of days from the past to reach the present, that individual cannot help but fail. Why? Because in an infinite regression of days, one could never move in reverse to the beginning of days or from the beginning to the present, because there exists an infinite number of days between the two points.[33]

---

[31] William Lane Craig and Paul Copan, *Creation Out of Nothing* (Grand Rapids: Baker Academic, 2012), 201–3.

[32] Robert J. Spitzer, *New Proofs for the Existence of God* (Grand Rapids: Eerdmans, 2010), 200.

[33] J. P. Moreland, *Scaling the Secular City* (Ann Arbor: University of Michigan, 1987), 29.

The (Theologically Informed) Cosmological Argument: Sermon Starter

One of the greatest shortcomings of this argument is that it proves the existence of a god, not the triune God revealed through the biblical canon. Moreover, we should find no comfort in the skeptic accepting the idea that a god exists. The skeptic already believed that prior to any apologetic explanation (see Romans 1). This argument by itself surfaces what the unbeliever already knows to be true: that they are created by a being beyond space and time. We want to use this line of reason in conjunction with explicitly Christian calls to repent and believe the gospel.

As is fitting within your preaching, use the cosmological argument to illustrate the existence of God. So often, those defending Christianity against skepticism seek to do so by first arguing for the existence of God. However, most mainstream apologetic arguments are meant to drive the skeptic to admit the existence of God prior to arguing for the Christian God. This approach is not entirely incorrect or ill-conceived; it may be particularly fitting to your context, geography, and demographic.

Still, we are convinced that when a skeptic moves from a materialist worldview to a general monotheistic worldview, this is not necessarily a victory. Embracing a fragile and unorthodox monotheism does not equate to an allegiance to Jesus. Transitioning from materialism to monotheism is an exchange of one false system for another.

As pastors, we must allow the apologetically rich narratives to be paradigms for our sermons. For instance, the Ethiopian eunuch was persuaded of his need for Christ from the scroll of Isaiah, and Paul preached about the resurrected Christ to the philosophers at Mars Hill. Likewise, the pulpit is an ordained space where theologically informed philosophy can prompt doubters into believing and embracing the anticipated Christ who defeats sin, death, and the grave. As we craft sermons, we recognize a skeptic's longing for redemption yet intentionally interweave theology and philosophy to irrupt these transcendent desires.

For example, if you are preaching on Genesis 1, Psalm 8, or John 1, consider using the cosmological argument to provoke the skeptic's imagination by inviting him or her to consider that existence must have a cause and thus has a beginning. These two premises are agreed on by the larger scientific community and the theological community. Exegeting or exploring Genesis 1–2, you might add, offers such a grand, cosmic explanation of how time and space come into existence simultaneously. Yet these two propositions within the cosmological argument yearn for an answer to the question, "If something does come from nothing, then who or what created all that is?"

You could then interweave the prologue of John's Gospel to demonstrate the intercanonical conversation that John has with the themes of Genesis 1–2. But note how John offers his hearers a christological spin: "In the beginning was the Word, and the Word was with God, and the Word was God" (John 1:1). And here is the gospel knot that John ties to his opening chapter: This Son is not only the eternal Word who coexists with the Father and the Spirit in the beginning; he is also a cocreator with the Father and the Spirit as each mysteriously generate a fecund energy of space—water, skies, earth—along with time—days, nights, seasons. And lastly, this eternal Son takes on flesh to "[take] away the sins of the world" (John 1:29). This paradigm is what we mean by a theologically informed cosmological argument because it entertains the philosophical angle of God's existence while supplying the theological angle of the person and work of the Son.

> **Notable Quotes:** "[In the person of Christ] a man has not become God; God has become man."
>
> _____
>
> Cyril of Alexandria (c. 375–444)

The Claims of Christ: Deity and Resurrection

Your congregation will be more familiar with the claims of Christ than any other apologetic issue. However, they likely need direction in piecing together the data and evidence for both the central claims of Christ regarding his deity and his resurrection. How you do this will be a pastoral task that trains and equips the church to give reasonable defenses for the hope within them. As we explore these two claims, we will review a few essential components to introduce to your congregation and then offer a few homiletical suggestions for your preaching.

The Claims of Christ: Deity

Skeptics of the New Testament are correct when they note that Jesus never says the phrase, "I am Yahweh in the flesh." The name "Yahweh" is derived from the four consonants of the revealed name of God in the Old Testament (YHWH, e.g., Exod 3:15), which is known as the tetragrammaton. However, the New Testament authors consistently identify Jesus as Yahweh, and even Christ's own words lead to the inevitable conclusion that he is Yahweh.

Theological Claim	Old Testament	New Testament
Creator	Isa 40:28	Col 1:15–17
The Judge	Joel 3:12	2 Tim 4:1
First and Last	Isa 44:6–8	Rev 22:12–13
Walks on Water	Isa 43; Ps 77	Matt 14:26–27
Occupies the Throne	Ps 110:1; Dan 7:13	Mark 14:62

In numerous passages in the New Testament, the religious elite, known as the Sanhedrin, were concerned about some of Jesus's own self-identity claims—especially found in John's "I am" statements (John 6:35, 41, 48, 51; 8:12; 10:7, 9, 11, 14; 11:25; 14:6; 15:1, 5).[34]

---

[34] Rather than attempt to reinvent the wheel, we will direct you to an easily quotable resource that, if purchased in digital form, could also supply some reproducible charts: Robert Bowman and Ed Komoszewski, *Putting*

And they became so infuriated with his statements that they sought his death because he seemed to be identifying himself with Yahweh.

For instance, in John 8:12–20, Jesus identifies himself as the true light coming into the world. As N. T. Wright notes,

> The idea of God calling someone to be the means of bringing light to the world is rooted in ancient Judaism. There, in the prophet Isaiah in particular, it is Israel who will be the world's true light. But, ultimately, it is the Lord's servant who is anointed to bring God's truth and justice to the world, and who at the climax of the book dies a cruel death to achieve the goal.[35]

In context, John depicts Jesus as the light of Yahweh's reign, and Israel (particularly, the Pharisees) as the darkness. The Pharisees' "behaviour, their attitudes and their ambitions indicated that they didn't know the one Jesus called 'father'; and that was why they couldn't recognize him as having come from this one true God."[36] This theological friction between Jesus and the Sanhedrin

---

Jesus in His Place (Grand Rapids: Kregel, 2007). This is an excellent overview of the case for the deity of Christ that is communicated in a manner that anyone can understand.

[35] N. T. Wright, *John for Everyone, Part 1: Chapters 1–10* (London: Society for Promoting Christian Knowledge, 2004), 116. Wright goes on to add, "The claim to be the world's true light, like so much that Jesus says in this gospel, is not in itself a claim to be divine (though John believes that, and wants us to believe it too)," Wright, 116.

[36] Wright, 117.

entangles the Gospels, climaxing in the Son's death to restore both Israelites and Gentiles, the chosen and the "non-chosen." The New Testament authors, like John, portray Jesus in numerous ways, and they certainly are not shy about depicting him with divine attributes.

Notable Quotes: "For they (the apostles) did not love the present age, but him [Jesus] who died for our benefit and for our sake was raised by God."

Polycarp (c. 69–155 AD)

In *When Did Jesus Become God?*, scholars Bart Ehrman, Michael Bird, and Robert Stewart attempt to map the origins of the deity of Jesus, ranging from Jesus's baptism, the resurrection, and the ascension.[37] The authors are trying to discover the answer to one fundamental question: "Does the New Testament indicate a deification of Jesus, or are they describing an always already deified Jesus?" Erhman suggests that the New Testament writers allude to the former (a term called *adoptionism*), whereas Bird and Stewart lean to the latter.

In his opening section, Bird humorously admits that Jesus never explicitly states, "Hi, I'm God, second person of the Trinity.

---

[37] See Bart Ehrman, Michael Bird, and Robert Stewart, *When Did Jesus Become God?: A Christological Debate* (Louisville: Westminster John Knox, 2022).

Soon I am going to die for your sins, and then I'd like for all of you to worship me."[38] Instead, he adds that the preexistence of Jesus is something the disciples "inferred from the resurrection because if Jesus has ascended into heaven, then in retrospect he must have descended in the first place. That could be the type of logic that is being employed."[39]

Careful scholarship, whether unorthodox or orthodox, is attentive to the nuances of the biblical text, and each of these scholars represents such academic prudence. Yet we side with Bird and Stewart because the New Testament canon seems to rouse the reader into confessing that Jesus is Yahweh in the flesh because of his preexistent nature, his sonship, his messianic title, his miracles, and his enthronement.

The Claims of Christ: The Resurrection

Admittedly, both of us are indebted to the simple yet powerful presentation of Gary Habermas's evidence for the resurrection of Jesus. His approach is called the "minimal facts argument." His argumentation exhibits the collectively agreed-upon data among scholarship, and as he notes, when this evidence is presented, it is perfectly logical to conclude that Jesus actually arose from the dead.

---

[38] Ehrman, Bird, and Stewart, 65.
[39] Ehrman, Bird, and Stewart, 85.

However, prior to presenting the minimal facts approach, we want to demonstrate that the claim of Christ's resurrection is early and ubiquitous in the Christian tradition. Paul's first letter to the church at Corinth was written in the early 50s AD. And Paul presents the facts for the resurrection of Jesus as the central claim of the Christian faith:

> Now I want to make clear for you, brothers and sisters, the gospel I preached to you, which you received, on which you have taken your stand and by which you are being saved, if you hold to the message I preached to you—unless you believed in vain. For I passed on to you as most important what I also received: that Christ died for our sins according to the Scriptures, that he was buried, that he was raised on the third day according to the Scriptures . . . (1 Cor 15:1–4).

Paul highlights that the most important message is the life, death, burial, and resurrection of Jesus from the dead. Additionally, this corresponds to the prophecies given, regarding the Messiah, throughout the Old Testament (the Old Testament being what Paul is referencing with "the Scriptures").

He continues with minimal, but effective, facts for his argument—a pattern followed by Habermas:

> And that he appeared to Cephas, then to the Twelve. Then he appeared to over five hundred brothers and sisters at one time; most of them are still alive, but some have fallen

asleep. Then he appeared to James, then to all the apostles. Last of all, as to one born at the wrong time, he also appeared to me (15:5–8).

Paul presents as evidence for the resurrection the testimony of the apostles (the Twelve), the 500 eyewitnesses (likely referencing the ascension of Jesus), to the former skeptic-turned-believer named James (the half-brother of Jesus), and then Paul himself (a former persecutor of the church). He then argues that all of the Christian life and Christian hope is bound up in this claim:

> Now if Christ is proclaimed as raised from the dead, how can some of you say, "There is no resurrection of the dead"? If there is no resurrection of the dead, then not even Christ has been raised; and if Christ has not been raised, then our proclamation is in vain, and so is your faith. Moreover, we are found to be false witnesses about God, because we have testified wrongly about God that he raised up Christ—whom he did not raise up, if in fact the dead are not raised. For if the dead are not raised, not even Christ has been raised. And if Christ has not been raised, your faith is worthless; you are still in your sins. Those, then, who have fallen asleep in Christ have also perished. If we have put our hope in Christ for this life only, we should be pitied more than anyone (15:12–19).

Notable Quotes: "Therefore, having received orders and complete certainty and caused by the resurrection of our Lord Jesus Christ believing the Word of God, they went with the Holy Spirit's certainty, preaching the good news that the kingdom of God is about to come."

Clement (c. 35–99 AD)

Without the resurrection of Jesus from the dead, Christianity falls. So understanding the basic evidence for the resurrection is critical for the health of a local church.

The minimal facts approach proposes four primary lines of evidence for the resurrection of Jesus:

1. Jesus died by crucifixion.
2. The tomb of Jesus was found empty.
3. The disciples were convinced he arose from the dead.
4. Skeptics became believers.[40]

Let's walk through each fact. First, the claim that Jesus died by crucifixion is nearly beyond contestation. Famous skeptics such as

---

[40] This method of argumentation is detailed in Gary Habermas and Michael Licona, *The Case for the Resurrection of Jesus* (Grand Rapids: Kregel, 2004).

Notable Quotes: "It is impossible that a being who had stolen half-dead out of the sepulchre, who crept about weak and ill, wanting medical treatment, who required bandaging, strengthening and indulgence, and who still, at last, yielded to his sufferings, could have given to his disciples the impression that he was a Conqueror over death and the grave, the Prince of Life, an impression which lay at the bottom of their future ministry. Such a resuscitation could only have weakened the impression which he had made upon them in life and in death, at the most could only have given it an elegiac voice, but could by no possibility have changed their sorrow into enthusiasm, have elevated their reverence into worship."

David Friedrich Strauss, *A New Life of Jesus*, authorized trans., 2nd ed., 2 vols. (London: Williams & Norgate, 1879), 1:412.

John Dominic Crossan,[41] Gerd Ludemann,[42] and Bart Ehrman[43] all acknowledge that the historical Jesus died on a Roman cross. Even

---

[41] A noted leader of the Jesus Seminar and a longtime professor at DePaul University.

[42] A well-known skeptic of the miracle claims of the New Testament, Ludemann served as professor of New Testament at Vanderbilt University.

[43] Well known for popularizing skeptical arguments about the veracity of the New Testament, Erhman serves as professor at The University of North Carolina (Chapel Hill).

the oldest non-Christian historical traditions assume that Jesus was crucified by the Romans.[44] For instance, the Jewish historian Josephus wrote, "When Pilate, upon hearing him [Jesus] accused by men of the highest standing among us, had condemned him to be crucified."[45] The notion that Christ was not crucified is relegated to old Islamic traditions[46] and hyper-skeptical positions but not among scholarship.

The second historical fact that must be addressed is that the tomb of Jesus was found to be empty. Now, the central claim of the Jewish leadership according to Matt 28:13–15 was that the disciples stole the body. However, this is implausible for a number of relatively obvious reasons.

First, the disciples were in hiding because they were wanted men. Second, are we to suppose that a band of unlearned Jews really overwhelmed armed and highly trained Roman soldiers? Of course not! So the Roman soldiers claimed that disciples came and stole the body while they were sleeping. This begs the question: How would

---

[44] In his satirical work, *The Death of Peregrine* (c. 150 AD), Lucian of Samosata wrote, "The Christians, you know, worship a man to this day—the distinguished personage who introduced their novel rites, and was crucified on that account."

[45] Josephus, *Antiquities* 18.64 (c. 94 AD).

[46] For a useful summary of this position, see Gregory Lanier, "'It Was Made to Appear Like That to Them': Islam's Denial of Jesus' Crucifixion," *Reformed Faith & Practice* 1, no. 1 (May 2014): 39–55, https://journal.rts.edu/article/it-was-made-to-appear-like-that-to-them-islams-denial-of-jesus-crucifixion-in-the-quran-and-dogmatic-tradition.

they know who stole the body if they were sleeping? If the soldiers were sleeping, surely the removal of a mutli-thousand-pound stone from the entrance of the tomb would have caused enough noise to wake up the soldiers. Third, in the disciples' recounting of the resurrection they describe female disciples finding the tomb first. In the first century, for a variety of cultural reasons that are difficult for modern readers to comprehend, the claim that women found the tomb first would have immediately rendered the claims of the disciples to be suspect at best. Last, once the disciples realized that claiming the resurrection of Jesus gained them nothing (e.g., no power, no prestige, no resources) and made their lives infinitely more difficult and dangerous, someone would have confessed to stealing the body. However, they did not. This claim was so laughable among early Christians that an early Christian historian, Eusebius (263–339 AD), mocked it in one of his publications:

> "Let us band together," the speaker proclaims, "to invent all the miracles and resurrection appearances which we never saw and let us carry the sham even to death! Why not die for nothing? Why dislike torture and whipping inflicted for no good reason? Let us go out to all nations and overthrow their institutions and denounce their gods! And even if we don't convince anybody, at least we'll have the satisfaction of drawing down on ourselves the punishment for our own deceit."[47]

---

[47] *Demonstratio Evangelica* 3.4–5.

William Lane Craig echoes Eusebius's assessment in his book, *The Son Rises*. He writes,

> The disciples could not have stolen the body from the tomb, had they wanted to. The Jews had set the guard around the tomb specifically to prevent theft of the corpse. The story that the disciples stole the body while the guard slept is ridiculous, for (a) how could the guards have known that it was the disciples who stole the body, if they had been sleeping? And (b) it is ludicrous to imagine the disciples' breaking into the sealed tomb and carting away the body while the guards were peacefully sleeping at the very door. Thus, the theft hypothesis is hopelessly impossible.[48]

In summary, the deist who holds to this theory must believe (1) that twelve poor fishermen were able to change the world through a plot laid so deep that no one has ever been able to discern where the cheat lay; (2) that these men gave up the pursuit of happiness and ventured into poverty, torments, and persecutions for nothing; (3) that depressed and fearful men would have suddenly grown so brave as to break into the tomb and steal the body; and (4) that these imposters would furnish the world with the greatest system of morality that ever was.

---

[48] William Lane Craig, *The Son Rises: The Historical Evidence for the Resurrection of Jesus* (Eugene, OR: Wipf & Stock, 2000), 27–28.

The retort to this could obviously be, "Well, what if Jesus didn't actually die? What if he just appeared to be dead?" This is a paraphrase of the largely defunct anti-resurrection argument known as the "swoon theory." The idea is that Jesus merely appeared dead on the cross and once placed in the tomb the cool damp air revived him, he awoke, and he escaped. This is largely comical for a variety of obvious reasons, but let us attempt to recount a few of the more absurd realities that must be overcome.

First, if Jesus merely swooned, how did he recover so quickly from a brutal whipping and crucifixion with enough strength to move a multi-thousand-pound stone from the opening of his tomb? This would have been incredibly difficult for multiple healthy men to accomplish, much less a single and nearly dead man. Second, upon moving his own stone, how would Jesus have stealthily navigated the presence of the Roman soldiers? Third, how would he have convinced the disciples he really overcame death if, at the risk of sounding crass, upon the examination of his wounds the injuries on his body would have still been mushy, bloody, and oozing? Fourth, if he was revived in the tomb, how did he accomplish all that we have just mentioned and take a roughly seven-mile walk with some of his followers on the road to Emmaus? The logical leaps necessary for the swoon theory to even resemble coherence are humorous in both nature and number.

The third and fourth facts can largely be handled together. The disciples were convinced that Jesus arose to the point that were willing to risk what little comfort they possessed in this life to proclaim the victory of Christ. While the earliest traditions regarding the deaths of the disciples vary, the early consensus is that most of the disciples died horrific deaths while preaching the resurrection of Jesus. People only die for claims they believe to be true.

The last factual claim that skeptics, such as Paul, became believers is quite persuasive. Imagine a contemporary figure like Osama bin Laden, a religious extremist and persecutor of the Christian faith, becoming a preacher of the gospel. The fervent Pharisee named Paul was known for his violence against and persecution of the church, yet he becomes a Christian par excellence; this is a remarkable story of transformation. Paul was deeply convicted in his religious tradition, and this spiritual background permeated his everyday life, from how he interpreted Scripture to his intense observation of the law to his persecution of all Jews who blasphemed Yahweh and his law. Thus, Paul must have experienced something so compelling on the road to Damascus that unhinged everything he dearly held as true. And that something must have been the resurrected Jesus.

In summary, the skeptic of the resurrection must provide an adequate explanation that remains consistent while rebutting the four lines of evidence for the resurrection of Jesus from the dead. The strongest conclusion is that Jesus arose from the dead.

The Deity and the Resurrection of Jesus: Sermon Starter

Building from our conclusion, we must envision how to implement potent explanations of the central claims of the deity and resurrection of Jesus for the skeptic in the pew. One necessary aspect of preaching is to acknowledge your audience, which means we must understand the skeptic's personal views, takes, and persuasions as we present evidence, examples, and explanations for the deity and resurrection of Jesus.

In his booklet *How to Reach the West Again*, Keller aptly demonstrates that most of the West, for centuries, assumed "a 'sacred order'—a transcendent, supernatural dimension of reality that was the ground of moral absolutes and promised life after death."[49] As you can tell in daily conversations with non-believers, this social imaginary of a sacred order is not how the West sees and perceives reality.

Nowadays, the epistemic default (how one has been taught to know reality) of the modern West denies a sacred order, where there "are no transcendent realities to which we must conform."[50] If the skeptic in the pew no longer assumes a sacred, divine order that can invade the present, horizontal order, then claims about the deity and resurrection of Jesus are nonsensical. The claim that

---

[49] Timothy Keller, *How to Reach the West Again* (New York: Redeemer City to City, 2020), 8.

[50] Keller, 8.

God takes on human flesh is a claim of the supernatural invading the natural, and the claim that Jesus was resurrected from the dead is a claim that the transcendent renews the horizontal. As Justin Ariel Bailey rightly states, the modern "imagination is being tasked with the burden of finding meaning in a flattened world."[51] Following Keller, we ask, "How, then, do you evangelize people who lack any sense of sin or transcendence, or who lack the traditional basic religious infrastructure such as belief in a Supreme Being or the afterlife?"[52] We could begin with the skeptic's own infrastructure.

If the skeptic supposes there is no transcendent realm beyond what can be experienced, offer homiletical bridges into topics such as beauty and justice. These two topics alone are welcoming ideas to the post-Christian imagination. Why? Generally speaking, most of American culture has an aesthetic longing for beauty, largely reinforced by videos on social media. Similarly, most Americans have an ethical longing for a just society—otherwise there would not be hot cultural topics revolving around race, economics, gun violence, and political corruption. In light of these two topics of beauty and justice, there is hope. No, really, hope is a predisposition of both beauty and justice. It is a genuine expectation of more than what we can see.

---

[51] Justin Ariel Bailey, *Reimagining Apologetics: The Beauty of Faith in a Secular Age* (Downers Grove, IL: IVP Academic, 2020), 25.

[52] Keller, *How to Reach the West Again*, 9.

Hope, according to both Rom 8:24–25 and 1 Cor 13:13, is a partial knowing of the future new creation. Paul bases this partial knowing on the resurrected Jesus. And building from this partial knowledge, hope anticipates something more, something really real, and something really good. The modern imagination senses something more in the topics of beauty and justice. Beauty and justice are recognizable yet fully unattainable, and we know this because we cannot seize, master, and bottle them. They are in our gaze but beyond it, leaving us longing for their fullness and complete revelation.

Can you get a feel for the skeptic's horizontal infrastructure now? For such individuals, they should begin feeling some "cross-pressures"[53] between their horizontal plane and an imposing transcendent plane. In other words, skeptics might have "underestimated the ability of disenchantment [a worldview without transcendence] to sustain significance."[54] They are hoping for another world, another realm, and another reality even when they cannot see, smell, feel, taste, or hear such a reality. Here is our long-winded point: There are cracks in the secular, horizontal plane, and the transcendent is invading our world. The skeptic's hopeful longings

---

[53] "Cross-pressures" is a term coined by philosopher Charles Taylor to describe how the modern self simultaneously experiences the pressures of transcendence within the horizontal planes of reality. See Taylor, *A Secular Age* (Cambridge: Harvard, 2007), 594–617.

[54] James K. A. Smith, *How (Not) To Be Secular: Reading Charles Taylor* (Grand Rapids: Eerdmans, 2014), 64.

for a better world reveal their predispositions for transcendence and a society drenched in moral perfection.

When we use examples like these from the pulpit, we are building an apologetic bridge. We are revealing a skeptic's already operational categories of transcendence in order to illustrate that the sacred order is not closed off to our horizontal, immanent, everyday world; rather, the "sacred" invades the "secular." Or as James K. A. Smith winsomely concludes his book, "In that cross-pressured space, some will begin to feel—and be honest about—the paucity of a closed 'take.' And in ways that they never could have anticipated, some will begin to wonder if 'renunciation' isn't the way to wholeness."[55]

As we preach, one of our apologetic goals is to invite skeptics to sense those cross-pressures and into a renunciation of a closed, merely horizontal field. Therefore, the claim of Jesus's resurrection is not, for the church, a mythological fairytale; it is a transcendent claim of God's reign penetrating the horizons of humanity, thus demonstrating that the sacred order is not only probable, it is also sensible here and now. In short, we are inviting skeptics to gaze on the transcendent Christ within the horizons of the mundane.

The Reliability of the Bible: An Introduction

Most objections to the claims of Scripture originate from skepticism over the reliability of the text. Was it copied accurately? Are

---

[55] Smith, 138.

the gospel materials from eyewitness accounts? Has the Bible been changed? You may not have enough time on a Sunday to answer those questions thoroughly in a sermon. However, you can speak to the issues in a way that equips your congregation.[56]

An entire field of textual criticism is dedicated to studying the Old Testament and its transmission. It would be beyond the scope of this book to engage that material extensively, so we will provide a shorthand summary of how you can speak to that issue without getting into the weeds, as it were: Jesus affirmed that the Old Testament text of his day was about him[57] and was Scripture. The Old Testament text of Jesus's day is materially the same as the Old Testament text in your English Bible[58] and is therefore a moot point. Jesus affirmed the historicity and the claims of the Old Testament, and he confirmed his deity and authority by his resurrection. Thus, we can believe his assessment that the Old Testament text is true, accurate, and authoritative. Additionally, during the second and third centuries, the early church uniformly recognized the Old Testament as divinely revealed Scripture.[59]

---

[56] A helpful resource to navigate these questions is Steven Cowan and Terry Wilder, eds., *In Defense of the Bible: A Comprehensive Apologetic for the Authority of Scripture* (Nashville: B&H Academic, 2013).

[57] Luke 24:44–47.

[58] As demonstrated by the Dead Sea Scrolls.

[59] Ronald Heine, *Reading the Old Testament with the Ancient Church* (Grand Rapids: Baker Academic, 2007), 32.

Notable Quotes: "We don't get to choose whether or not something is true. We don't *invent* truth. We don't determine it. We search it out and accept it with gratitude, even when it's at odds with our feelings or preferences."

Brett McCracken, *The Wisdom Pyramid: Feeding Your Soul in a Post-Truth World* (Wheaton, IL: Crossway, 2021), 61.

The Reliability of the Bible: The New Testament

The New Testament opens with the four Gospels.[60] These accounts speak to the life, ministry, and salvific work of Jesus that are the defining theological commitment of the Christian faith. Each of these books presents its material as being based on the eyewitness testimony of those who knew Jesus personally. This may not be obvious to English audiences, but textual scholars have long noted that each gospel account gives a nod or reference to its source material in one form or another.[61] The Gospel of Mark appears to be

---

[60] Irenaeus spoke of the fourfold Gospels in the same way that he spoke of the Old Testament being Scripture. *Against Heresies* 3.11.8.

[61] An excellent resource detailing this material is Richard Bauckham's *Jesus and the Eyewitnesses* (Grand Rapids: Eerdmans, 2017). Another helpful resource is Craig Blomberg's *The Historical Reliability of the New Testament* (Nashville: B&H Academic, 2016).

based largely on testimony from Peter, Matthew is largely his own recounting of the life of Christ, John's account comes from his own personal interaction with Christ, and Luke bases his material off of interviews with a number of eyewitnesses to the life and miracles of Jesus. Thus, the Gospels constitute eyewitness testimony to the life of Christ.

The remainder of the New Testament is attached to someone who knew Jesus personally, with the only exceptions being Acts and Hebrews. Acts is the second book penned by Luke, who acts as an investigative journalist by interviewing those who witnessed the birth of the church and the spread of the gospel in the ancient world. The authorship of Hebrews has long been debated even though it was widely accepted as a canonical book in the early church. Even speaking of books being debated raises the question, "When was the content (canon) of the New Testament decided or settled?"

First, the content of the New Testament was not decided at the Council of Nicaea (325 AD) as many skeptics like to claim. Instead, Nicaea was called to reaffirm the orthodox teaching that Jesus is eternally coexistent and coequal with God the Father. This was meant to correct the rapidly growing influence of the Arius (256–336 AD), who taught that Jesus was created.[62]

---

[62] A thorough interaction with the events surrounding the Council of Nicaea is found in Lewis Ayers's *Nicaea and its Legacy* (Oxford: Oxford University, 2004).

> **Notable Quotes:** "The evidence for our New Testament writings is ever so much greater than the evidence for many writings of classical authors, the authenticity of which no one dreams of questioning. And if the New Testament were a collection of secular writings, their authenticity would generally be regarded as beyond all doubt."
>
> ———
>
> F. F. Bruce, *The New Testament Documents: Are They Reliable?* (Grand Rapids: Eerdmans, 2003), 10.

Second, the rise of heresy in the early church did lead to churches independently identifying which books were Scripture.[63] Throughout the ancient world, churches separated by geography, culture, and language all used a very similar process to identify which New Testament books should be viewed as Scripture. No council was appointed to determine the criteria; this was a true grassroots effort, superintended by the Holy Spirit.

———

[63] For instance, an early heretic named Marcion (85–160 AD) began circulating highly edited versions of New Testament books in order to establish his own version of Christianity, influenced by Gnosticism. Individual churches were forced to respond by delineating which books were Scripture and which were not.

- *Criteria One: Apostolicity*—If a book or letter could be traced to one of the apostles, it was immediately considered to be Scripture.
- *Criteria Two: Orthodoxy*—The content of a book letter had to fit theologically with what was taught in the Gospels and the Old Testament.
- *Criteria Three: Antiquity*—If a book or letter entered into circulation long after the death of the apostles, such as is the case with the so-called gnostic gospels, it was rejected. A book or letter had to be circulated within the lifetime of the apostles.
- *Criteria Four: Catholicity*—If a book or letter was rejected by a church that had direct association with the apostles, other churches would follow suit. Again, this was informal in nature but nevertheless did occur.[64]

This process of identifying what books or letter were inspired by God was critical because of the amount of persecution being faced by the early church. In short, if you were going to be punished for owning, reading, or quoting from sacred texts, you needed to be sure they were in fact sacred.

What about the accuracy of the transmission of the New Testament manuscripts? How do we know that what we possess is

---

[64] An academic discussion of these criteria and much more can be found in Lee Martin McDonald's *The Biblical Canon* (Grand Rapids: Baker Academic, 2006).

what Jesus said? Certainly, critics such as Bart Erhman[65] have developed quite a lucrative following in claiming that the sheer number of New Testament variants, some estimates placing the number around 400,000, demonstrates that we do not actually know what was written in the original copies of the New Testament. Numbers like this are staggering until you understand the context.

First, we have 400,000 textual variants because we have an incredible number of manuscripts (more than 5,700). The more manuscript data you have, the more textual variants will be present.

Second, the overwhelming majority of these variants are inconsequential. For instance, a large number of them are due to spelling errors (like dittography) or word order differences.

Third, only a few hundred words in the entire New Testament are up for debate, and none of them pertain to a central Christian doctrine.

In fact, fewer variants would lead scholars to question how much the text of the New Testament was controlled and edited. The abundance of variants speaks to its veracity, not against it, which is why Christians gladly produce books and entire catalogs[66]

---

[65] Bart Ehrman, *Misquoting Jesus: The Story Behind Who Changed the Bible and Why* (San Francisco: HarperSanFrancisco, 2007).

[66] Phillip Comfort, *New Testament Text and Translation Commentary* (Carol Stream, IL: Tyndale, 2008). These variants are not hidden. They are available to any person who wants to learn more about them: https://www.logos.com/product/144301/textual-variants-collection.

of the variants for study and scholarly inquiry. In short, the New Testament textual tradition is robust and reliable.

Notable Quotes: "Besides textual evidence derived from New Testament Greek manuscripts and from early versions, the textual critic compares numerous scriptural quotations used in commentaries, sermons, and other treatises written by early church fathers. Indeed, so extensive are these citations that if all other sources for our knowledge of the text of the New Testament were destroyed, they would be sufficient alone for the reconstruction of practically the entire New Testament."

Bruce Metzger and Bart Ehrman, *The Text of the New Testament: Its Transmission, Corruption, and Restoration*, 4th ed. (New York: Oxford University, 2005), 126.

The Reliability of Scripture: Sermon Starter

As we have noted several times so far, skepticism pervades the American consciousness. It can be both a gift and a curse. As a gift, it can keep us sharp and prudent; as a curse, it keeps us insulated and naïve to ideas and beliefs outside our perspective. Skepticism has (epistemic) limits; it is great for asking probing questions but is typically unsuccessful in answering such questions. So pastors have a difficult task of penetrating naïveté to open up a skeptic's worldview to offer a better account of the evidence.

For instance, and pertaining to the reliability of Scripture, many ask the very questions with which we opened this section, such as "Was the Bible copied accurately?" and "Are the gospel materials from eyewitness accounts?" If these are the questions skeptics are asking, ask them from the pulpit. Do not dismiss them, but rather entertain those serious inquiries and share how you may have posed the same questions early in your Christian walk. By doing so, you are offering a tangible paradigm of faith, seeking understanding.

For instance, when we ask questions from the pulpit, we exhibit humility. One of the greatest dangers of any Christian is to assume he or she knows everything about every topic of Scripture. Knowing everything is not possible, and it is idolatrous. To be like God is not the same as being God-like. As the Proverbs remind us, "Fear of the LORD is the beginning of wisdom" (Prov 9:10). Old Testament scholar Daniel Block writes that fear is a "trusting awe of a superior."[67] We are contingent creatures of God, so we are dependent on his self-revelation to know him and his world rightly.

Similarly, when we ask questions from the pulpit, we exhibit how faith seeks understanding. As much as modernity tries to persuade us, we cannot untether ourselves from our worldviews and see

---

[67] Daniel I. Block, *For the Glory of God: Recovering a Biblical Theology of Worship* (Grand Rapids: Baker Academic, 2014), 9.

reality unbiasedly.[68] We must not fall prey to the view that we must take off our faith in order to know the world rightly.[69] In his essay "What is the Enlightenment?" the German philosopher Immanuel Kant suggests that one of the tenets of Enlightenment thinking was to remove itself from the "tutelages" of religion. In other words, Kant believed that religion polluted rationality. Following the early church since Augustine, we herald that faith births understanding, and such knowing is funded from within the bounds of Scripture as well as a local body—where preaching and liturgy fruitfully foster rightly ordered love and knowledge.

Lastly, when we ask questions from the pulpit, we exhibit that hard questions require arduous examinations. In our digital age, information is at our fingertips, but not all information should be treated equally. The word *research* has been flattened and made banal. Research, for most Americans, means that we explore a topic for under an hour on irreputable websites. Encourage skeptics to

---

[68] Our view is that there are healthy and unhealthy biases. Healthy biases lead to faithful understandings of reality, whereas unhealthy ones develop into unfaithful understandings of reality. A healthy bias, we could say, is to perceive Earth as designed, ordered, and thus created by God. This echoes William Lane Craig's cosmological argument. An unhealthy bias would entertain that Earth is not designed, ordered, and created. This position is less tenable because it must now entertain how life is seemingly ordered and not chaotic, meaningful and not meaningless.

[69] For a brief blog post on Kant and the role of faith, see Michael McEwen, "Reason Within the Bounds of Liturgy," Center for Baptist Renewal, October 30, 2018, https://www.centerforbaptistrenewal.com/blog /2018/10/30/reason-within-the-bounds-of-liturgy.

seek comprehensive answers for their questions and not simplistic ones that confirm their biases. Since the discovery of the Dead Sea Scrolls, the topic of the reliability of Scripture has garnered enormous amounts of scholarship, and thankfully, it is one with a multitude of resources to dive in to. We would encourage you to study the topic alongside skeptics, because this encounter can grow into a more personal apologetics.

Conclusion

As you use apologetics in your preaching or teaching, remember your two primary audiences (believer and unbeliever) are composed of those who are bent toward deep intellectual engagement and those who require popular-level explanations. Therefore, be clear in how you communicate. Do not muddy the water with academic jargon meant to impress those who are well read. Speak clearly and effectively.

State something in a way that demonstrates you have considered it in a manner consistent with great intellectual rigor, but then immediately restate it in a way that does not belittle those in your audience who require simpler explanations. When I (Dayton) state something academically and then restate something in a way that the entire audience should be able to understand, I usually introduce this explanation with something like, "And you already know what I am saying because you . . ." and then point at a way in which they already use a concept such as the law of non-contradiction or the logical implication of moral absolutes. When you encourage your audience in these ways, you will draw them in and give them confidence. Effective apologetic communication is clear, winsome, saturated with grace, accessible to your audience, and ultimately calls people to do something with the truth claims of Jesus.

Heart Work (Reflection Questions)

1. What apologetic issues are you avoiding in your preaching and why?

2. If you do avoid certain issues, is that avoidance caused at all by fear, either of your own inability to tackle the issue well or of how your listeners may respond?

3. What are you actively doing to be better prepared to address apologetic issues in your preaching?

4. What apologetic issues need to be addressed in the next thirty days?

Chapter 4

Apologetics in Your Church

Most people in America, when they are exposed
to the Christian faith, are not being transformed.
They take one step into the door, and the journey
ends. They are not being allowed, encouraged,
or equipped to love or to think like Christ.
—DAVID KINNAMAN AND GABE LYONS[1]

T he pulpit will determine whether the church body reclaims
the task of Christian apologetics. This chapter assumes that
the preaching ministry has adopted some of the guidance of chapter

---

[1] David Kinnaman and Gabe Lyons, *UnChristian* (Grand Rapids:
Baker, 2007), 82.

3. If not, the following material will produce much less fruit than it could and should. In the last chapter, we teased ideas for you to develop pertaining to theological topics and themes from the pulpit. In this chapter, we will offer more practical ideas. Preaching on particular apologetic topics may come easily for most pastors, yet the behind-the-scenes training may be more difficult to implement. So we will propose a few modes and models for implementing and practicing apologetics from within the contexts of the local church, from training to classes. The reader should see these equipping moments as opportunities to buttress our Sunday preaching and teaching. The suggested classes and trainings in this chapter could be used as more personal times for theological discipleship, as advantageous occasions for ecclesial shepherding.

Worldview Formation

I (Dayton) pastor Redeemer Church in North Carolina, and it is largely in a rural context. The nearest large Christian institution of higher learning is roughly an hour away at Southeastern Baptist Theological Seminary. The majority of those who make up our church membership are blue-collar workers with technical training. While we do have some with advanced education, primarily in the medical field, like most congregations in America our demographic is essentially composed of hard-working people with little time for research and academic engagement. What they learn regarding apologetic issues (for good and for bad) is primarily consumed passively through mass media or social media. In the digital age, accusations against the trustworthiness of Scripture, the claims of Jesus, and objective moral values have been relegated to thirty- to ninety-second sound bites with dramatic music, quick camera cuts, and authoritative tones from those who claim expertise. This methodology is highly effective in shaping the assumptions, beliefs, and doubts of entire congregations.[2]

The response of the church must be to once again priortize formative disciplines that prepare and teach congregants how to think. This is not a quick process; most things of value take time. Instead it is a lengthy and time-consuming effort to shape worldviews. So be committed for the long haul.

This is a necessary undertaking because, as James Sire notes, everyone has a worldview that shapes every area of thinking from the mundane "Where did I leave my watch?" to the profound "Who am I?" Every question is answered through a worldview.[3] The question then is how is the local church shaping worldviews in general? While that is beyond the scope of this book, certainly shaping

---

[2] We must regularly remind our congregations that they are being formed by the world around them into believers of something. The question is simply, "What is that 'something'?" We are either being passively formed and shaped or actively formed and shaped. Christian formation, especially in the realm of worldview and discernment, requires ongoing, intentional efforts toward formation.

[3] James Sire, *The Universe Next Door* (Downers Grove, IL: IVP Academic, 2009), 19.

worldview as it relates to addressing apologetic issues in culture is essential to shaping and forming a right worldview.[4]

What we want to lay out in this chapter is not a one-size-fits-all template for incorporating apologetic training and worldview-building efforts in every church. It is, however, the approach that is bearing fruit in our very normal church, in a very normal context, with very normal people. In short, we do believe that some contextually varied version of our approach would be effective in most churches.

> **Notable Quotes:** "For all our cynicism, we are—at the end of the day—inescapably creatures of hope. We look forward; we yearn for something more, something better—anything to give meaning, value, and substance to our short lives."
>
> ——————
>
> Douglas Groothuis, *Christian Apologetics: A Comprehensive Case for Biblical Faith* (Downers Grove, IL: IVP Academic, 2011), 15.

---

[4] One aspect of worldview formation that should be reclaimed in the Western world is the inherently supernatural view of reality that is present in the Scripture. See Rebecca Manley Pippert, *Stay Salt: The World Has Changed, Our Message Must Not* (Epsom, UK: The Good Book Company, 2020), 66–67. "The biblical view of reality embraces both the seen and the unseen. What is seen is only part of the world, but the unseen reality—the supernatural presence of God, the Holy Spirit, angels, and demons—is viewed as even more real!"

Apologetic Training

Redeemer Church is intentionally simple. We gather on Sundays, and we scatter during the week to live our lives on mission and to meet in small groups for mutual encouragement. The aim is to only gather for a limited number of hours per week so that they can spend the bulk of their time living out their identity as missionaries. However, a few years ago we noticed a gap in our ability to effectively build biblical literacy and to shape worldview, so we launched The Redeemer Institute. Our institute acts as a kind of Christian education ministry within our church.

Our institute has a partnership with Southeastern Baptist Theological Seminary to provide opportunities for class credit for those who would like to eventually pursue more formal training. While a partnership like this is a blessing, it is not necessary to accomplish the end goal of training.

We offer opportunities for brief (usually seven to twelve weeks in length) but rigorous Bible studies over short books of the Bible or even a single chapter. Additionally, we provide core classes that resemble a seminary course with a syllabus, textbooks, reading schedules, class projects, and lengthy lectures. For some, the classes are a daunting first step, so we host single-evening events that have a speaker on a specific subject, speaking on a popular level, with light refreshments and even free resources (e.g., books) available. All of this is meant to be part of the process of shaping and forming people's hearts and minds. We will explain how each of these elements function together.

Apologetic Classes

We ask people to register for classes through our website, just like they would if they were participating in a seminary setting. Once registered, they pay a small fee to cover the cost of their books. We have found that paying for textbooks provides the necessary incentive for people to prioritize the totality of the courses. We usually offer one book that would fit the description of a traditional textbook, while the accompanying book is more of a popular-level treatment of the class subject.

In our current format, the class gathers for a few lectures per semester, and each lecture lasts approximately two hours. At the end of each class there is an opportunity for questions and answers. Further, those teaching each class make resource suggestions (e.g., books, podcasts, videos, blogs) during each lecture to continue to supply congregants with the tools they need to grow. For our apologetics class we follow this outline for content:

1. What is apologetics?
2. What is the apologetic mandate?
3. How do I know God exists?
   a. The moral argument
   b. The cosmological argument
   c. The transcendental argument
4. How do I know that Jesus is the Messiah?
   a. The claims of Jesus (a case for his deity)

      b. The evidence for the bodily resurrection

  5. How can I know that the Bible is trustworthy?

      a. Manuscript history/the canon

      b. An interaction with skeptics (Bart Erhman and others)

      c. Internal consistency

      d. Church history

  6. Apologetic issues and evangelism

      a. Hot-button cultural issues

      b. How to engage skeptics

      c. Sharing the gospel while navigating questions

      d. A call to gospel living

The aim with this course is to regularly remind those in the class that the end goal is not to develop a clever or snarky response to the office atheist or the uncle who comes to Thanksgiving and makes fun of your faith. The goal of the class is to be equipped and grow in confidence as we submit to the Holy Spirit's leading for the purpose of removing roadblocks to faith. We start our first class session by writing down on a whiteboard the name of an unbeliever that each student wants to engage in a gospel conversation prior to the end of the semester. Throughout the course we pray over those names. Similarly, our class assignments are largely centered around students reflecting on how to best summarize what they are learning in a way that they could share it with a skeptic over a cup of coffee. The purpose of the class is not information consumption; it is missional mobilization.

Single Events

For many, the idea of registering for a class elicits flashbacks of dimly lit high school hallways, microwaved pizza lunches, and those marbled notebooks we all used in school. To put it bluntly, taking a class is not something many people want to do voluntarily. This is where a single-evening event that incorporates worship and a time for community could be a strong on-ramp to more rigorous training.

We have held single-evening events with great success. For example, after a few weeks of promoting, we hosted an event at night that explored the minimal facts approach to arguing for the historicity of Jesus's resurrection. We coupled it with worship, a time for community, snacks, and childcare, and we kept the lecture portion to thirty minutes. From that we offered an opportunity to go further by taking the apologetics class through our institute. A few dozen people registered for classes out of that event.

We have also held events where we brought in a noted speaker or expert on a topic and had them speak for thirty minutes, followed by an on-stage interview that interacted with what they taught. Then we gave everyone in attendance a copy of the expert's book with a call to go further in one of our classes. What we found is that a very high number of those in attendance, at the very least, read the donated book.

A basic outline for one of these events could be something like this:

1. Welcome and overview to the evening
2. Worship through song
3. Lecture/teaching (thirty minutes)
4. Follow-up interview (optional, fifteen minutes)
5. A call to go further with a class (a clear action step is necessary)
6. Dismiss to time of fellowship

A well-planned event such as this could stir interest to go deeper in studying apologetic issues (or any subject for that matter).

Apologetic Drip

If you have ever experienced water damage in your home, you know how far a steady drip can spread. A consistent drip is soaked up by what it is dripping on and fundamentally changes the composition of whatever that object is. While this is a negative example, what if the opposite were true? What if a consistent drip did not change something for the worse but strengthened it into something better? We believe that in the context of the local church, a consistent apologetic drip will have a positive and lasting impact on the congregation. The key is the consistency of the drip. Regardless of how this could occur in your context, apologetic preaching and teaching will only go so far if the drip is not regular and strategic throughout the ministry of the church.

Apologetics: I (Dayton) would recommend casually demonstrating how to think logically and critically throughout your preaching. This could include random or seemingly unforeseen critical engagements of the text of Scripture. For example, during our Genesis sermon series, when I began to talk about the flood of Noah's day the audience naturally began to ask questions about the veracity of the account. So I stopped mid-sermon and casually pointed out that regardless of the debates surrounding the timing (the age of the earth) and scope of the flood (whether it was global or universal), looking for Noah's ark as evidence for the flood is a fool's errand at best. Following the destruction of the flood, solid timbers for the construction of homes, fences, stables, and barns would have been in high demand. The one place to find those supplies would have been the body of the ark itself. Therefore, logic demands that the ark would have been dissembled by Noah and his family to be repurposed into homes and shelters for livestock. Including details like this in your sermons will help your people to think more carefully about what they are reading and hearing.

There are a variety of ways to drip apologetic training and worldview shaping throughout the ministry of your congregation. For example, have book-giveaway Sundays. At key times of the year, we have worked out deals with publishers (most are very willing to be generous with discounts for churches) to buy a copy of a book for every member household of our church. Sometimes these have been focused on cultural issues that require a Christian response, and at other times they were simply resources to encourage spiritual growth. Regardless, while many people will not use the resource, those that do will benefit from it. Through this steady drip of solid resources, we have witnessed sustained growth and increasing interest to engage in more rigorous training (even in the area of apologetics) in our church family.

Another opportunity is through selling books at a steep discount. Again, at key or strategic times of the year, we purchase resources in bulk and sell them at a loss just so our church can have access to a book that is of great value. Often these books have been on apologetic issues. Regardless of our cost for the book, we sell it for five dollars. The purchase price (much like the class registration price) adds motivation to actually read the content of the book. It has been a fairly common occurrence for someone to buy a book from our bookstore, read it, and then ask how they can learn more.

Depending on your church's ministry structure, there are some simple ways to reinforce what has been said about an apologetic subject during a Sunday morning sermon. Redeemer Church has sermon- or text-based small groups that meet weekly. These groups gather in homes to discuss the text that was preached on Sunday to highlight important takeaways. The group leaders are given discussion guides with commentary or prompts to help them navigate the group discussion. These discussions are primarily calls toward confession of sin, pursuing holiness, resting in grace, and practically applying insight from the text of Scripture.

However, if an apologetic issue is addressed on a Sunday, it will be highlighted in the discussion guide for our groups. This ensures a fertile format for remembering and wrestling with a specific apologetic issue in the context of gospel community. Often these moments of wrestling, in the context of community, have been used by the Holy Spirit to bring clarity for those in seasons of doubt or confusion. For others, these conversations have served to embolden them to engage their friends, family, neighbors, and coworkers who are skeptics.

In summary, the faithful restoration of apologetics to the local church context must include the pulpit, the classroom (formal training), communal wrestling (e.g., small-group discussion), open invitation (e.g., events designed to stoke interest), and consistency (the apologetic drip).

Heart Work (Reflection Questions)

1. How are you intentionally building your own worldview into what rightly views and prizes Christ?
2. In what ways are you actively and strategically shaping the worldview of your congregation?

3. What avenues currently exist to train Christian thinkers in your congregation?

4. What will you initiate in order to more effectively train the members of your congregation?

5. What is one thing you can do in the next thirty days to put these steps into action?

EPILOGUE

There are a dozen views about everything until you
know the answer. Then there's never more than one.

—C. S. Lewis[1]

E nvision with us a nation full of churches that act as cultural
exegetes and speak the truth in love. Congregations who are
ready to reason with the unbelievers around them, to contend for
the faith, but to do so with gentleness and respect. As the West
increasingly lurches toward secularism, it will become necessary for
every Christian to be prepared to give an answer for the hope that
is in them. Is your church prepared? This is not a question about
the church being prepared for the future; it is about the present.

---

[1] C. S. Lewis, *That Hideous Strength* (New York: Scribner, 1996), 70.

The lurch is in full force, and the local church has much ground to recover in its cultural witness.

Parachurch ministries are wonderful tools that can and should exist in order to support initiatives of the local church, but they must never take the place of the local church or its scriptural mandates for engaging the world. For far too long churches have relied on professional apologists, slick websites, branded videos, and snarky memes to do the heavy lifting of engaging our world with a reasoned defense of the gospel.

We are convinced that this restoration of apologetics to the local church begins with a right understanding of the rule and reign of King Jesus. To restore apologetics to the local church means beginning with restoring our understanding of Christ as King. It is only once we have become thoroughly convinced of the rule and reign of Christ as King that we can faithfully and persuasively appeal to unbelievers with the audacious claim that we are citizens of a better kingdom with a better king.

What good are our arguments apart from our faithfulness? What good is a shrewd turn of a phrase without a selfless turn of kindness? What good are sound answers without humble living?

To borrow a phrase from the late Francis Schaeffer, how then should we live? Like Jesus is King. How then should we speak? With clear answers, kind hearts, good reasons, and good intentions. The local church is God's plan to reach the nations, preach the truth, and defend the faith once and for all delivered to the saints.

Do you believe it?

Heart Work (Reflection Questions)

1. What areas of your life are not under the reign of King Jesus?
2. In what ways does your church reflect or not reflect the rule and reign of King Jesus?
3. What can you do in the next thirty days to better live under the reign of King Jesus?

APPENDIX 1

Liturgical Apologetics

Introduction

We want to invite you to consider your services as an opportunity for apologetically equipping your congregation and engaging your neighbors. For the purpose of this book, we will use Easter Sunday as a test case for how you could engage the congregation with an eye toward apologetics.

Weeks in advance you encourage your congregation to identify their one—the one person they intend to bring to Easter Sunday. You have printed attractive invitation cards, online you have boosted video invitations that have been shared on various social media platforms, you have posted high-quality posters throughout your community in the hope that one of these media will engage someone who is curious about Jesus.

And it worked.

A Story

A recent college graduate named Ryan has been invited by his neighbors, and he repeatedly watched your Instagram reels. Easter Sunday, he is awake and ready to go, but he has not been to church since his grandmother took him to vacation Bible school as a child. He is not against the Christian faith, he has just heard so much from his professors and his classmates about the absurdity of Jesus's claims and the closed-minded behavior of his followers. Still, what could it hurt to attend an Easter service with his neighbors?

As Ryan pulls into the parking lot, he is surprised to see a parking team ready to welcome him and help him find a parking space. As he exits the car his hears "Good morning" from a member of the parking team. He awkwardly responds, "Hi," as he makes his way to the building. His neighbors are waiting outside for him, and after some brief pleasantries, they walk toward the entrance. The door greeters shake everyone's hand with excited exclamations of "He is risen!" only to hear many people who are entering the building reply with "He is risen indeed!" This exchange catches Ryan off guard. He asks his neighbors why everyone is saying the same thing. Ryan's neighbors explain that it is a traditional Christian greeting on Easter Sunday to proclaim and affirm that Jesus really did rise.

As Ryan meanders through the lobby, he is greeted by the smell of freshly brewed coffee. He wonders how much it costs. Then he notices that everyone is filling their cup without paying for anything. As Ryan fills his cup, various strangers greet him and introduce themselves. He is surprised by the friendliness from people who are so very convinced about things that the culture finds so strange.

> **Notable Quotes:** "A faithful, Christ-centered church and its wisdom-infusing patterns of worship are increasingly a refuge for those being pummeled by the maelstrom of our digital era."
>
> McCracken, *The Wisdom Pyramid*, 88.

After filling his cup with coffee, Ryan follows his neighbors into the worship center to find seats. As they are seated, he notices a QR code on the chair back in front of him that says, "Get Connected." He pulls out his phone and scans the code. It opens a landing page that tells him how to learn more about the church and its ministries, and then it briefly explains what he will experience during the service. The music playing throughout the worship center turns down, and someone walks onto the stage and greets everyone with the now familiar phrase, "He is risen!" Most of the room, now including Ryan, responds, "He is risen indeed!" The host of the service then laughs and explains, "If this is your first Sunday, that was probably

weird, but that confession is why we gather here today. We are convinced that Jesus conquered the grave, and so we have hope and
salvation. Now, let's stand together and sing to the risen King!"

The entire room stands as the band begins to play. Ryan
dreaded this moment. He does not really listen to Christian music.
But just a few seconds into the song, he is struck by how familiar it
sounds. "Oh wait, I've heard this before," he thinks to himself. The
band intentionally chose to start the service with a song that those
who are unchurched might be familiar with. With people like Ryan
in mind, the band began playing a popular song from the radio,
"Graves into Gardens." While he does not know all the words,
Ryan remembers enough to feel comfortable to sing a few lyrics.
As the song ends, the worship leader asks everyone to take a seat.

As the room is seated, two men stand near a water trough that
has been placed in the corner of the stage. A pastor named Todd
introduces himself and explains what is about to take place: "For
those who are new, we are about to witness a baptism. Baptism
is a public declaration of allegiance to Jesus as our King. It sym-
bolizes his death by being buried in the water, and it pictures his
resurrection by rising from the water. What you are seeing is the
public witness of a life that has been changed by the gospel." Ryan
is intrigued; he has never seen a baptism in person.

A video begins playing with a woman named Alice detailing
her life before Christ and sharing her story of coming to faith in
Christ. She describes the moment she believed the good news of

Jesus in her place. Ryan is struck by how she describes the gospel: "Jesus in my place." The video ends, and Alice is plunged under the water and rises to the raucous applause of the room. Pastor Todd then speaks to the room, to people like Ryan, and invites them to repent and believe the gospel, like Alice has.

As Pastor Todd steps off the stage, the band comes back and invites people to stand again, and then the worship leader carefully and kindly invites the audience to sing the next song by explaining that each phrase in the chorus reminds us of the hope we have in Jesus. As the congregation sings "Hallelujah for the Cross," Ryan initially struggles to follow along. However, by the second chorus, he is comfortable and at least mumbles along. As the song ends, the band leader prays.

Pastor Erik walks onto the stage and greets the room with, "He is risen!" Now, Ryan is ready and responds, "He is risen indeed!" As Pastor Erik greets the crowd, Ryan is surprised by the feeling in the room. This is not a stuffy lecture or a rote religious ceremony, but the pastor and congregation seem genuinely convinced that Jesus is alive. Pastor Erik reminds the room that the human heart longs for hero stories. It is why Americans have invested years and money into watching the Marvel franchise unfold its tapestry of stories. Ryan was surprised by Pastor Erik's command of Marvel movie knowledge and his references to the sacrificial death of Tony Stark. Then things take a serious turn: "Tony Stark's sacrifice tugs at our hearts because written on your soul is a longing for a hero who defeats an undefeated foe. That hero is Jesus, and the enemy he defeats is the grave." As Ryan sits surprised at the Christ figure motifs that Pastor Erik highlighted from his favorite movie franchise, he could not help but wonder where the sermon was headed.

As Pastor Erik is about to begin his exposition of John 20, he says, "Here is the big idea today, the one thing I want you to take home with you: Jesus is alive, and death is defeated." That statement was clear enough, but it struck a chord. Ryan has experienced his fair share of grief and loss. So he was curious how Pastor Erik would speak to the issue of death.

Starting in the opening verses of John 20, Pastor Erik notes that the first people to reach the empty tomb were women. Much to Ryan's surprise, Pastor Erik stops and says, "And if you were making this story up, that is the worst thing you could have contrived. As backwards as it may seem, the testimony of women wasn't even allowed in a court of law. It was a cultural assumption that women lie. I know that's offensive, but it was just the context of the day. So this is an embarrassing detail in the account of the resurrection. It would not have made the story more believable, but less. It is details like this that cause even the most die-hard skeptics of the resurrection to admit that the first disciples were convinced that Jesus arose from the dead." Ryan is shocked by not just the absurdity of not allowing women to testify in court rooms, but by the fact that the Gospels included this detail if it would hurt the Christian cause.

As Pastor Erik continues, he highlights that Peter and John ran to the tomb together, but that John went out of his way to highlight that he got there first: "In short, teenage boy John wanted everyone for all of history to know that he was faster than that cranky middle-aged fisherman named Peter. And this is typical of John and Peter's relationship. In the Gospel accounts you see these two men are together a lot, and they tend to give each other a hard time. Guys, just like you like to tease and joke about your best friends, so did John and Peter. It's why John highlights that when he saw the empty tomb, he immediately knew what happened and Peter remained perplexed. He wants you to know he is faster than Peter in body and mind. These are the kind of relational details that only make sense if this is an eyewitness account." Ryan has never had the text of Scripture humanized like that. He always thought of it like a thirdhand account, not eyewitness testimony.

As Pastor Erik makes his way through John 20, Ryan grows more conflicted. He is very interested by what he is hearing, but he has so many doubts that he begins to feel as if he should not even be in the worship service. Then Pastor Erik highlights Thomas. Jesus had appeared to the other disciples following his resurrection, but not Thomas. When Thomas heard that Jesus arose from the dead, he thought that the other disciples were playing a trick on him. He refused to believe what they said, until Jesus appeared to him. Pastor Erik explains, "When Jesus appeared he offered his wounded body as proof that he really had conquered death. Thomas examined the body and then exclaimed, 'My Lord and my God!'" Pastor Erik peers through the crowd and says, "This is a safe place to wrestle with doubts and ask hard questions. Jesus isn't afraid of your doubts. Jesus isn't offended by your questions. When a father approached Jesus, asking for healing for his son, Jesus told him that all things were possible for the one who believed. The father responded with, 'I believe, but help my unbelief.' Your doubts and your questions are welcome here. Jesus has the answers you're looking for."

Ryan feels like Pastor Erik is speaking directly to him. And then when Pastor Erik shares, "Jesus told the disciples, blessed are those who do not see and still believe. Congregation, that's you." Pastor Erik finishes his sermon by explaining the good news of the gospel: Jesus's perfect life, his substitutionary death, and his resurrection from the dead. He summarizes it as "Jesus in my place." Ryan has never heard it explained in this way. He is intrigued but not ready to believe. Pastor Erik reminds the congregation one final time, "Jesus is alive, and death is defeated! We have hope. The grave cannot hold us!"

As the sermon ends and the band returns to the stage, another pastor walks out and asks those trusting in Christ to take the communion cups from the chair back in front of them. He explains that this was only for believers, that this meal was to declare the work of Jesus to express our common-union, or communion, with Christ and with one another. Ryan feels awkward, but he does not take the communion cup. His neighbors assure him, "It is okay. This is for those who know that they believe. You are welcome here whether you believe or not."

As communion ends, the band begins to play the next song. Ryan is entirely unfamiliar with the song. "It is Finished" by Matt Papa is one of the favorite hymns of the church, and people all around Ryan sing loudly of the finished work of Jesus. While he is not ready to believe, Ryan is moved to see hundreds of people passionately confessing the same truths in song. As the song ends, the worship leader invites the congregation to read aloud with him the Apostles' Creed: "Let's confess together what we believe. Jesus was resurrected from the dead and he is coming again. Read this aloud with me." As the congregation reads the creed out loud, Ryan stands silent. He does not want to confess to believing something that he is unsure he actually believes. As soon as the creed ends the band rolls into one more song, "Death Was Arrested" by North Point Worship. It is a celebratory song about death's defeat. Ryan wishes he could have the confidence of his neighbors, who clearly believe that Jesus is alive.

As the song ends, the worship leader says, "Listen, if you came today because someone invited you, we are glad you joined us. This is a safe place to ask hard questions, to wrestle with doubt, and to find truth on two legs: Jesus of Nazareth. We'd love to have you join us next Sunday or stop by our next steps table to learn about ways you can get good answers to hard questions." After a brief word of benediction from the end of John 20, the congregation is dismissed.

Ryan makes his way to the next steps desk and picks up a first-time guest bag. He is not ready to ask hard questions, but he feels welcomed. As he walked to the car, his neighbors thank him for coming. They then ask if he wants to come the next Sunday. He responds, "Yeah, I think I could do that." Intrigued by what he heard, a winsome gospel presentation that wove answers to hard questions throughout the sermon, he begins to wonder if there is something to the claims of Jesus.

While this narrative is fictional, throughout the lifetime of Redeemer Church we have witnessed numerous stories like this of men and women who were skeptical to the claims of Jesus. They came to one of our services that were constructed with an eye toward winsome apologetic engagement, and the Spirit moved. Either they repented and believed during the service, or it began a journey toward faith. Regardless of the when and how of salvation, the point is to structure our services in such a way that the skeptic and doubter are engaged with the good news of Jesus.

A Sample Plan

The easiest service on your church's calendar to plan with an eye toward apologetic engagement is Easter Sunday. We will provide a sample plan and order of service that you could use. It must be contextualized to your church and city, so, for example, some of the songs will need to change. However, the guidelines contained in narrative form (such as starting the service with a song many unbelievers might know) remain true, regardless of your context.

Communication

We urge you to strategically plan your preaching calendar around an intentional build-up to Easter Sunday. That does not mean that each spring's preaching series is the same. It just means you have in mind how you will naturally transition from your current series into Easter Sunday. For example, my (Dayton's) church spent about six months in the Book of Genesis. I strategically planned to cover in the weeks leading up to Easter the portion of Genesis that deals with the life of Joseph. We titled that portion of Genesis, "The Son Who Saves." I highlighted all the ways that the life of Joseph foreshadowed the life of Jesus.[1] It provided a natural off-ramp from a book study to Easter Sunday as a stand-alone sermon and evangelistic and apologetic event. If you plan the preaching calendar with Easter in view, it becomes an easy avenue by which to begin communicating the importance of Easter Sunday.

We encourage you to pick an Easter theme, visual style, Sunday sermon title, and so on that are not overly "churchy." Stay with punchy themes like "Death is defeated" or "Resurrection = Restoration."

---

[1] I detail how to preach the life of Joseph in a way the foreshadows Jesus: "Preaching the Life of Joseph," *Bible Study Magazine*, July/August 2020, 30–33.

Aim for something that will grab the attention of your congregation, skeptics, and church dropouts.

Work with one of the many affordable graphics and communications firms for churches to finalize your visual communication style, and then set up video and picture ads on Facebook, Instagram, and other social media platforms. Print invitation cards and mini-posters that can be used for verbal invitations. You might even consider a unique URL and landing page for Easter that details everything that will happen that morning so that first-time guests know what to expect.[2]

Begin running social media ads and encouraging verbal invitations six weeks from the date of Easter Sunday. At the one-month mark, instruct church members to formally ask their one to attend with them. Two weeks from Easter, they should ask again or confirm that their guest is coming. Then, the Sunday before Easter, your congregation should finalize details with their one. They should confirm what time and where they will meet to go to services together and be prepared to answer all questions that might arise.

The key to all of this strategy is prayer. Two months prior to Easter Sunday, call on your congregation to pray for the one person they intend to invite to Easter. In the weeks leading up to Easter Sunday, take a moment during each pastoral prayer and as

---

[2] I (Dayton) have found this to be very helpful as we engage our community. Our Easter URL is https://www.RockyMountEaster.com

a church ask God to prepare the hearts of unbelievers, doubters, and skeptics to hear and believe the good news that will be shared on Easter Sunday.

Now, for Easter Sunday, here is a suggested outline based on what has been effective and Christ honoring in the life of Redeemer Church.[3]

Welcome

Have an excellent communicator host your service. They should welcome the church body as a whole with first-time guests in mind. That means they should quickly and winsomely explain everything that is taking place. For example, "Good morning, we are so glad you are here today. If you are new, take the guest card in the chair back in front of you, and please fill it out. We do not want you to feel pressured to give an offering later; instead we ask that you just let us get to know you. Drop the card in the offering box, and our pastor will send you a note in the mail, thanking you for gathering with us today. Today is a great day. We are celebrating that Jesus is alive and death is defeated. We will celebrate that through singing songs,

---

[3] If you have never considered the strategic planning of services with a specific liturgy in mind, I (Dayton) would commend to you the work of the Center for Baptist Renewal for whom I serve as a fellow, and we provide a number of resources, including sample liturgies, to help churches begin to adopt a mindset of careful intentionality with their service structure. The sample liturgies are available at https://www.centerforbaptistrenewal.com /sample-liturgies.

sharing testimonies during baptism, hearing what we believe about Jesus during Pastor Erik's sermon, and inviting you to respond. We are so glad you're here today. Let's stand and sing together."

Song 1

Pick a song that might be familiar to a casual Christian radio listener. This is an effort to help ease guests into the service with something that might be familiar. Our church is contemporary, so the example I used in the story was "Graves into Gardens." If your church is more traditional you might choose a hymn that is widely known like "Amazing Grace." The aim is to start with something familiar so that your guests will be increasingly at ease and ready to hear and believe.

Corporate Reading or Baptism

Pick a corporate reading that ties to the text being preached. If you are preaching John 20, it could be the angel's proclamation that Jesus is risen or Thomas's confession of Jesus as Lord and God. The point is to direct your congregation's hearts toward the truth they are about to receive and to show unbelievers that these are things we confess to be true together. If you have someone being baptized on Easter Sunday, placing the baptism early in the service sets the tone and communicates that the gospel is a call to repent and believe. You can place additional baptisms again after the sermon if you have multiple baptisms and move the corporate reading until after the preaching.

Song 2

Pick a song that prepares hearts for the Scripture that is to be preached. For example, in the narrative above, I listed "Hallelujah for the Cross." This song works for both contemporary and traditional church settings.

Pastoral Prayer

I (Dayton) always acknowledge my sinfulness in my prayer before the sermon and ask God to save sinners in our midst. One of the most disarming things a pastor can acknowledge is his own sinfulness. This makes a big impact on skeptics, unbelievers, and those who feel shame for their sin and do not know what to do about it.

Sermon

My (Dayton) introduction usually plays heavily on cultural concepts that both believers and unbelievers are familiar with and then presents a problem that needs to be addressed. Carefully craft your introduction and know it cold. You want this portion of your sermon to feel the most conversational in tone and to pull the listeners into what they are about to hear from God's Word. I (Dayton) am a big proponent of transitioning to the text of Scripture by giving the audience a single "Big Idea" that anchors the entire sermon. A Big Idea should be short, clear, and memorable so that anyone (child or adult) can recall it on command. A short phrase is ideal, but a full sentence can work. If it is two sentences in length, nobody will remember it. Preach through the passage with the unbeliever in mind. Speak to the questions of skeptics casually by weaving answers to their questions throughout the sermon. However, you must avoid straw man or snarky statements. Do not mock their questions or act defensive. Calmly, clearly, and kindly engage issues as you work your way through the text.

After the Sermon

Coming out of the sermon, be explicit with what you are asking unbelievers to do: "Consider the claims of Scripture. My job is to tell you the truth. The call for you is to repent of sin and trust Jesus in your place. If you have questions about the gospel or the claims of Jesus, our pastors will be located _____ during the next couple of songs and available to talk after the service. This is a safe place for broken people; this is a safe place for hard questions."

Song 3

Here should be a song that targets the hearts of believers. For instance, "It Is Finished" by Matt Papa has excellent reflections on who Jesus is and what Jesus has done. In a traditional church setting, a song like "Jesus Paid It All" would be an excellent choice. The point of this is to raise the believer's affections for Jesus and to allow unbelievers and skeptics to witness this song of reflection and thankfulness being sung by God's people.

Communion

We take communion every week to declare what we have heard and believe is true about Jesus in our place. Use this time to explain the gospel clearly once again. As you invite believers to take communion, urge skeptics and unbelievers with language like this: "For those who are yet to believe, do not take communion, take Christ. We would love to talk to you about that." Then, once again, highlight where they can go to ask good questions about Jesus. Be very explicit in what is and is not happening in the Lord's Supper. Avoid insider language, and make it clear that communion is the gospel news made visible through a physical, tangible act.

Song 4

The final song of the service should be a declarative song of joy and confidence. For instance, "Death Was Arrested" reinforces the Big Idea of the sermon and further illustrates the difference that the resurrection of Jesus makes. In a traditional setting, a good song might be "Because He Lives."

Benediction

This is a great place to reaffirm a central point of hope from the passage in a way that illustrates the difference belief makes. Coming out of the resurrection account it could be as simple as reaffirming the Great Commission. Because Jesus arose, we are sent. Believer and unbeliever alike should be released from the service with one final reminder of the difference that Jesus's resurrection makes.

Thinking through your services with apologetic engagement in mind is not difficult; it just requires intentionality. Begin with next Easter's services, and then work from there to flesh out an ongoing strategy to build apologetic elements into your Sunday service planning.

APPENDIX 2

Building Your Apologetics Library

One of the first steps to take in incorporating apologetic equipping and practices into the local church is for the pastor (and the church leadership as a whole) to be well-versed in apologetic methodology and issues. The following will help you to be better equipped.

Classic Texts

C. S. Lewis, *Mere Christianity*
Francis Schaeffer, *How Should We Then Live?*
Francis Schaeffer, *The God Who is There*

Timothy Keller, *The Reason for God*

Augustine, *The City of God*

General Texts/Cultural Apologetics

Steven Cowan, ed., *Five Views on Apologetics*

Norman Geisler, ed., *The Big Book of Christian Apologetics* (encyclopedia)

Paul Gould, Travis Dickinson, and Keith Loftin, *Stand Firm*

Joshua Chatraw and Mark Allen, *Apologetics at the Cross*

Peter Kreeft and Ronal Tacelli, *Handbook of Christian Apologetics*

Rebecca McLaughlin, *Confronting Christianity*

Rebecca McLaughlin, *The Secular Creed*

Paul Copan and William Lane Craig, eds., *Come Let Us Reason*

Paul Copan and William Lane Craig, eds., *Contending with Christianity's Critics*

Paul Copan and William Lane Craig, eds., *Passionate Conviction*

J. P. Moreland, *Scaling the Secular City*

Scott Sunquist and Amos Yong, eds., *The Gospel and Pluralism Today*

Worldview Texts

Justin Ariel Bailey, *Reimagining Apologetics*

Justin Ariel Bailey, *Interpreting Your World*

William Dyrness, *Christian Apologetics in a World Community*

Paul Gould, *Cultural Apologetics*

Paul Gould, *A Good and True Story*

Hak Joon Lee and Tim Dearborn, eds., *Discerning Ethics*

J. P. Moreland and William Lane Craig, *Philosophical Foundations for a Christian Worldview*

Ronald Nash, *Worldviews in Conflict*

James Sire, *The Universe Next Door*

R. C. Sproul, *The Consequences of Ideas*

Presuppositional/Covenantal Apologetic Texts

Greg Bahnsen, *Always Ready*

Greg Bahnsen, *Van Til's Apologetic*

Greg Bahnsen, *Presuppositional Apologetics*

John Frame, *Apologetics*

K. Scott Oliphint, *Covenantal Apologetics*

Cornelius Van Til, *Christian Apologetics*

Cornelius Van Til, *The Defense of the Faith*

Classical Apologetic Texts

William Lane Craig, *Reasonable Faith*

Normal Geisler, *Christian Apologetics*

Norman Geisler and Frank Turek, *I Don't Have Enough Faith to Be an Atheist*

R.C. Sproul, *Defending Your Faith*

Evidential Apologetic Texts

Gary Habermas and Michael Licona, *The Case for the Resurrection*

Gary Habermas, *Risen Indeed*

Michael Licona, *The Resurrection of Jesus*

Josh McDowell, *The New Evidence That Demands a Verdict*

Cumulative Case Apologetic Texts

John Feinberg, *Can You Believe It's True?*

Douglas Groothuis, *Christian Apologetics*

NAME AND SUBJECT INDEX

SCRIPTURE INDEX